With [illegible]

in the

Moment

Enjoy the Moment!

Marcus D [illegible]

Marcus Batterbury

With You in the Moment

A Memoir

atmosphere press

Published by Atmosphere Press

Cover design by Matthew Fielder

Maya Angelou quote source: www.goodreads.com

Atmospherepress.com

For Guy, my Dad,
who is the true hero of this story.

Table of Contents

"I've learned that people will forget what you said, people will forget what you did, but people will never forget how you made them feel."

MAYA ANGELOU

Part One

Prologue

Leaving on a Jet Plane

I am standing with my parents in an airport lounge watching through the window as the plane leaves the runway and rises into the air. Without the sound effects, this massive lift against gravity appears effortless. The plane is ascending in silence and weightlessness. My inner spirits rise and soar along with the aircraft. Then, for a fleeting moment, a pause in time, it seems to be going too slowly, far too slowly, slow enough in fact to slip backwards out of the sky, and illogically down to earth, delivering its passengers back to the ground and back into our lives. Life in reverse, and a microsecond of internal panic. Then basic physics and common sense intervene. I blink and refocus. Thankfully and miraculously, it's just the plane continuing its assent in that unconfident way they often do when you are watching them.

At achieving altitude, the aircraft gracefully, and now powerfully, turns west. West towards another country and another continent. I reflect and realise my confidence and sense of positivity is already growing. This is actually happening. There were no delays takeoff was a success, and now the plane, along with its occupants, is heading away from us at over 500 miles an hour. Now, that is a great feeling.

As we turn from the window, the realisation that this event is over physically works its way up through my body, eventually reaching my aching cheeks that rise into a genuine smile. Something that hasn't happened for a while.

With what I sense is a shared feeling of relief, we make our way through the terminal and find a café where we order coffee and cake. Sitting down, I feel a sudden release in my stomach and chest. I am elated. I want to celebrate and sing out "Thank God that's over! They're gone! They're gone! Hoorah!" But I am not 100% sure of how my parents are feeling about this situation. So, I play it cool, act casually, and opt for our family tradition of people watching while making inappropriate comments.

My mum, not mentioning the departure but always curious, is studying the people around us. Wondering, in the moment, who they are, where they are going, or where they have just returned from. She shares her observations with us. "Look at those two. They look so happy together...I bet they are both married and having an affair."

"Mum! What makes you say that?"

"Well, look at his shiny shoes; he's definitely trying to impress her. And look at the way she's swinging her handbag!"

I accuse her of spicing things up.

She continues, and zooming in on somebody else says, "Look at that woman's shoes."

I subtly turn my attention in the direction of the unfortunate pair of shoes under scrutiny. I see innocent-looking, sensible, flat-soled footwear, well-polished but a little scuffed. Other than that, nondescript.

"She's definitely been a nun in a convent; I wonder what she's up to?" says Mum.

I look at her incredulously and then make an irresistible reference to *The Sound of Music*, and assume this woman is running away from her holy order and planning to shack up with a handsome single dad.

Then she is left speechless as a woman walks past pulling a pink suitcase, which matches her pink shell suit and what look like pink fluffy slippers. She says nothing, just gawps at the footwear.

"What is it with you and shoes?" I ask.

"You can tell a lot from people's shoes," she says, her eyes following the vision in pink.

I'm smiling. My wonderful parents sit before me – we have reverted to kind and are making up stories about strangers. We must be OK. It is strange that we are not talking about the last few weeks we have spent entertaining the guests that we have just said goodbye to. Maybe we are just trying to normalise things and take it all in our stride. Although on the face of it, it doesn't sound like a big deal, the truth is that this event has been massive and very impactful in all kinds of ways – but maybe if we don't speak about it in that manner, if we don't over-dramatise it, it will just go down in history as a small ripple rather than a colossal and potentially destructive wave.

After another half an hour, we have finished our coffee, eaten our cake, and run out of footwear to discuss. So, we head for the car park – let's go home.

* * *

Driving around the M25, my mum is, as usual, centre stage. She is sitting in the passenger seat next to my dad, who is driving, and I am sitting behind him, watching her, and listening to what she is saying. I'm sure I can detect an energy in her voice that signifies a newfound freedom. I think I can anyway.

She is talking about how "Amazing" it was that our visitors had just "Turned up out of the blue! With no warning at all! Just a call from the arrivals hall at Heathrow Airport!"

"Surprise! We've come to stay with you for a while; can you come and get us?"

She turns to my dad. "I couldn't believe it! And neither could you, Guy." He is agreeing, but with a quizzical look of surprise, wondering what she will say next.

Clearly, we are now at a safe distance in space and time

to, at least, acknowledge the visit, even if it is through the light-hearted and humorous filter that Renee Batterbury, my mother, is putting on it.

"We panicked, didn't we, Guy!?"

Not waiting for an answer but looking over her shoulder at me, she nods towards her husband and says, "As soon as he put the phone down, your dad headed for the airport to collect them, and their *masses* of luggage." She puts a special emphasis on the word *masses*. "When he saw how much they'd brought with them he wondered how long they were planning on staying, didn't you, Guy!" My dad has no time to answer and concentrates on driving.

Now on a roll, she continues, "While your dad drove to collect them, I stayed at home, cleaned and tidied the house, made up the beds, laid out towels, then I went out shopping to make sure they had plenty to eat – because they eat *masses* of food, don't they, Guy!" (Again, the emphasis on masses.) I tell her she did a great job getting it all sorted out at such short notice and add that I certainly couldn't have done it myself. Enjoying the praise, she continues, "It was brilliant really; just think a month ago we had no idea they were coming, but they did, and we all had a lovely time, didn't we, Guy?"

At each unexpected twist and turn in this conversation, my dad glances in the rearview mirror, and he and I have momentary eye contact, just a subtle acknowledgement of what is going on, and how we are handling it. I look at Mum as she continues speaking. She is full of it, smiling and laughing and obviously happy and proud of what has been achieved.

Right now, she is feeling good about herself, her place in our family, and what she and my dad have pulled off with next to no notice. And throughout this conversation, both Dad and I are right there with her, celebrating this unexpected and unplanned yet triumphant event. We are with her in the moment.

* * *

This all sounds, and feels, quite natural. Just a family, on the road home after dropping some visitors off at the airport. Happy that the visit took place without a hitch, relieved that everybody enjoyed themselves, but pleased that we can now calm down and get back to our day-to-day lives. And this, of course, is true.

However, despite this varied, entertaining and above all normal conversation, it's useful at this point to say that something else is going on here – a kind of confirmation for myself and my dad. You see, many of the details that are being described didn't actually take place. Other than the fact that we had visitors from overseas, the circumstances, the specifics, and the surprise that both my dad and I are validating in our conversation with Mum are not true.

The fact is, at the time of this journey, in September 2006, my mum is in the early stages of dementia, and to be more specific, most likely Alzheimer's disease.

* * *

The traffic slows and eventually we are stationary. No forward motion on a motorway feels so unnatural; it's like somebody has pressed pause and time is standing still.

My initial feeling of relief following *lift off* has faded and now, inside, I am asking myself, could this really be happening to my wonderful mum, and my dad's beautiful wife? Can she not remember the long and difficult buildup to this visit? Has that whole six-month period really disappeared from her memory? It's certainly not a part of her truth as she recalls it right at this moment. But are we doing the right thing by validating what she is saying, or will our actions just result in mixed messages and more confusion? I'm pretty sure both Dad and I are also wondering if this alternative truth and disappearing period of time is an indication of what is to come. Are we experiencing what life will be like from this moment on?

As I contemplate this, a small and familiar fist of fear clenches in my chest just behind my sternum and ribs. I feel emotional, a little scared, and my mouth is watering as it often does when I am feeling anxious or powerless.

Again, I catch my dad's eye in the rearview mirror, but this time we linger a little longer. There is a subtle difference in our connection and what we are communicating with our eyes. There is a kind of rawness and vulnerability. For a moment we have shown our true feelings to each other...or at least I think we have. I hope this is just my imagination and that he hasn't sensed my inner turmoil. I really hope he is OK, but I know I wear my heart on my sleeve – as does he – so we both find it a struggle to hide what we are really feeling, even if our outward behaviours are saying something quite different.

Momentarily I think about this, recognising that although on one level my dad and I are very much in it together, there is something else far deeper happening, and that is our own individual internal response to what we are seeing and hearing. Then I glance towards my lovely mum, and I am reminded that this isn't just about me and my dad – this is about all three of us, and moving forwards, there is a need for us to support each other through whatever the future holds.

I become aware that without noticing, my mind and imagination have stepped into the dangerous world of *what ifs*. I am catastrophising and inventing futures that do not exist. Recognising this, I find that I have gone from enjoying our journey home, listening to my mum's amazing stories and versions of the truth, to feeling overwhelmed with what the future might look like. I really haven't got the space in my head for this; it's not helpful and not healthy. So, I shake myself out of it, slam the door shut on those useless and baseless thoughts, and step back into the moment.

At last, the traffic has cleared, and we are on the move again, and despite this short dip into a less optimistic world of traffic jams and *what ifs*, in the true spirit of respect and love for the wonderful human being who is my mum, I am now continuing to join her in her reality.

On reflection, on this occasion, as with many others, her version of the truth is the most important, and a lot more fun and positive than mine – so why not go with her and take the road less travelled?

Rose-Tinted Specs

When I originally decided to write this book, I thought that its purpose would primarily be to record my parents' experience of living with my mum's dementia and, in addition to this, what we as her family and support network did, and put in place, to enable her to continue to live her best life. The hope being that learning from our trials, errors, successes, and mindset may provide people facing similar issues with some top tips, some reassurance and, most important, the confidence to see this illness through a more positive, hopeful, and manageable lens.

But as I began to write, memories and emotions washed over me that were so strong, relevant, and real that they affected my ability to speak objectively about their experience, without bringing my own thoughts and perceptions into the equation. When exploring significant events and milestones that took place during the journey into living with Mum's dementia, I realised that my only point of reference was my own story of living with her dementia. It was this combined view that informed my awareness of what was taking place and shaped my version of the truth.

In addition to this, it soon became clear that there are many other significant people, such as partners, family, and friends who also play key roles in this story. Their lives, like mine, are intrinsically linked and intertwined with my parents, and they will, no doubt, make appearances throughout this book.

But whoever we are talking about, what I would say, is that my dad's drive and unwavering love for his wife have inspired us all to keep our eye on the prize and place her wellbeing and enjoyment of each day at the centre of all our thinking.

As you continue to read, you will notice that it almost feels as if I'm seeing things through rose-tinted specs, and in some ways, I suppose I am. I'm writing about somebody I love very much who happens to have been living well with dementia for several years. My mum is a person of passion and energy, who grabs life with both hands and makes the most of any situation on any given day. As well as this spirited and open-armed approach to life, she also has what I would describe as a very determined and headstrong, if not stubborn quality, and as you will discover, it is the combination of these characteristics that have shaped the way she has chosen to live her life, both before and after the onset of her illness.

We know from what we read in newspapers, find on the internet, or see on TV that living with, or supporting somebody to live with dementia isn't easy. It can be a very challenging, emotional, frightening, and difficult experience for all involved. But, despite this, there can also be moments, or even long periods, of joy, humour, love, and inspiration, and it is these invaluable and life-affirming events that I have written about in this book, because they have proved to provide me and my family with an essential sense of hope and optimism for the future.

Dementia is an umbrella term used to describe several brain diseases, and although each of these has particular signs and symptoms, it would be fair to say that they can show up in different people, in different ways. So, to a certain degree, facing any kind of dementia can feel like approaching unchartered territory, with many possibilities and many unknowns. And, of course, wherever there are unknowns there is also the tendency to become fearful, and to get caught up in *what ifs*. This is natural, it's a part of the human condition, and, if I'm honest, when it comes to my mum's situation, on many occasions I fall foul of this tendency, and find myself in a spiral of negative and unhelpful thoughts. Although I can't say that I have discovered any quick wins or techniques to overcome these issues, I have noticed that over time, as my knowledge of her dementia and my self-awareness has improved, so has my ability to cope with the situation and to keep things in check.

But I am speaking from a position of privilege, because I also have a couple of bonus tricks up my sleeve that help me achieve and maintain the right mindset for most of the time. The first is the informed, pragmatic, and loving support that my partner, Simon, provides to me and my parents. Although he is a key and much-loved member of our family, when necessary, he is also able to step back a little from any situation and see things for what they are, and in doing so help us to get things in perspective and to move forwards with confidence. We know that he has our best interests at the centre of his thinking, so he can help us see the bigger picture, keep our eyes on what is important, and plan accordingly. I cannot overstate how valuable Simon's support is, and I do realise how fortunate we are to have him and his advice on tap whenever we need it.

The second trick I have is not so much up my sleeve, but instead it can be found in my genes. You see, being my mother's son, I am more than a glass-half-full kind of guy. One of the central themes of this book is the idea that we are all a product of our environment, and the environment I have been brought up in by both my parents is one of optimism and making the most of any given situation. This has resulted in me having a predisposition to see life through a positive and at times humorous lens, and it is through this lens that myself and my family proactively endeavour to deal with my mum's illness, and it is also through this lens that I have written this book.

So, although there is a great deal of information available about the challenging and difficult side of living with dementia, you will not find much of it in these pages. Instead, I am focusing on the other side of the experience – the joyful, loving, and respectful side that isn't spoken about and celebrated as often as it should be, because, in our individual situation, these positives far outweigh the negatives many times over.

To be clear, I am not saying that we do not struggle with the many issues and complexities that arise due to Mum's illness, because we do. And I am not saying we have all the answers or that we have a track record of doing the right thing all the time – as that would be a far cry from reality. This is not about preaching a right or wrong way of doing things; I'm just telling our story in the hope that it will be helpful. Everybody experiences and deals with things in their own way and, in this book, I am sharing my family's unique experience, which is, as you will see, driven, guided and, to be honest, dictated by the woman herself. So, I make no apology for those rose-tinted specs I am looking through; they belong very much to Renee Batterbury, my mother.

Our Windmill

We are continuing our journey home from the airport and, noticing a lull in the conversation, my dad turns on the car stereo. Johnny Mathis is singing "L-O-V-E" a favourite song which is usually sung by Nat King Cole, but we prefer Johnny's version. This journey could not get any better! Mum turns to me and sings the first two lines, and I join her in a duet for the rest of the verse. We know most of the words and guess the rest, which is all part of the fun and makes us laugh. If Simon was with us, he would be making up his own *blue* lyrics; he can always be relied upon to lower the tone and make us feel as if we are on the set of a *Carry On* film.

Johnny Mathis is just one of the many crooners who provide the theme music to our story, and he is always welcome to unknowingly interrupt our conversation and influence our thinking. His voice and this song are just one small part of the elaborate soundtrack that has been ever present in our family life; it's part of the glue which connects our network of memories, stories, and emotions. The glue which holds us together. We can always depend on our favourite tunes to put a smile on our faces, connect with significant people and events, and perhaps even get one or two of us singing...apart from my dad, of course, who wouldn't sing if you paid him.

On this occasion the song triggers a string of recollections for Mum, who is now describing she and my dad sitting in the front row of the London Palladium, back in the 1970s, seeing Johnny Mathis singing live, in concert, for the first time. What a magical experience! Unlike her memories of what has taken place over the last few months, her recollection of this event is crystal clear, and she recounts every step in detail, remembering the sights and sounds, smells, clothes and, crucially, what Johnny said between songs. In addition to this, ever the storyteller, she is adding a few embellishments for effect.

"He looked right into my eyes and winked, didn't he, Guy?"

After sixty years of marriage, my dad knows that when his wife finishes a sentence with one of those questions, he is required to back her up, even if she is going off script and adding a bit of sparkle to a tale.

As she describes the concert, Mum is conveying not only what she saw and heard, but also the emotions she felt throughout the evening. Emotions such as excitement, love, attachment, and the feeling of privilege at being a part of such a wonderful event. Recounting this, her enthusiasm and passions fill the car; they are vibrant and infectious. I feel as though I am there with her in the front row of the London Palladium on that magical evening, and maybe, just maybe, Johnny is winking at me... Yes, in fact I'm sure he is!

My mum's memories of this event match Dad's almost perfectly. I use the word *almost* because, as I have already said, she does have a life-long penchant for exaggeration and elaboration, which must not be mistaken for dementia. She just likes to tell a good story. In addition to this, I must point out that at the time of this first of many concerts, she was openly and madly in love with Johnny, whereas my dad just *quite liked* him, so maybe the emotional element of the experience was different for each of them.

As a side note – I remember when Johnny Mathis admirably came out as gay; my mum was far more surprised, and a lot more put out, than when I told her that I was. I'm not sure what I took from this, but looking back it does remind me what an exceptional and supportive mother she has always been, encouraging both her sons to live their best life. It also reminds me just how strong her romantic ambitions were for Mr. Mathis – she was not giving up on him, and his being gay was just a minor hurdle.

One of the main symptoms of Mum's illness is her diminishing ability to remember and retain recent experiences and information; this is known as short-term memory loss, and to a degree can account for her differing version of events related to our recent visitors. However, at this point, her long-term memories are more accessible and solid. So, the distant past is a comfortable place for her to anchor many of her conversations – hence her describing the concert in London with such clarity and feeling.

* * *

We are now turning onto the A12 and heading north-east. Mum is having a great time, sharing her memories and her thoughts, while also reading out and pointing to road signs for familiar towns which indicate we are heading home.

"Chelmsford!"

"Colchester!"

"Clacton-on-Sea! ...Don't miss the turning, Guy."

My dad responds to each of these announcements automatically because, more recently, this has become a regular occurrence. He is aware of the significance of what she is doing, and so he ensures his responses have an air of gratitude. He is subtly saying that he values her support. While this is happening, Mum is also reading number plates and the signs on the side of lorries and vans. Noticing how she managed to read the branding on the side of a van which quickly passed us, I comment, genuinely amazed, on her ability to *read at speed.* She enjoys this praise. She has always been proud of her reading abilities, and for that matter also of her eyesight.

My comment triggers another memory, and she is now telling us about her teacher at school saying, "You are a great reader, Irene (Renee), and if you continue to read, Irene, you can do anything you want with your life."

We are familiar with this anecdote. She tells it regularly; the words may differ, but the meaning is the same. Her teacher believed in her ability to read, and she has cherished that belief throughout her life. My dad and I respond as if hearing this for the first time, asking open questions that will enable her to go into detail and connect with other stories that make her feel good.

She pipes up again, "Careful! Careful! Watch those children, Guy, they might run into the road...Wherever are their parents?"

I know this passenger-seat driving must be winding my dad up. I imagine it's on the tip of his tongue to say, "I can see the bloody kids, I've got eyes; just let me drive the car!" But admirably he controls whatever he is thinking and remains light-hearted and positive.

As we near home the conversation dies down and, as if it had been pre-arranged, Louis Armstrong's "What a Wonderful World" is playing on the stereo. As we listen to this, we are each spending time in our own personal world of thought while watching the beautiful Essex countryside slide past.

When she spots the giant and slow-turning wind turbine that acts as a landmark to tell us we are home, Mum says, "There's our windmill, Guy!"

* * *

Later the same day, I am spinning the pedals of my bike, heading north along the coast from my parents' house towards Frinton. I love cycling on days like today. I have a tailwind, so I'm not needing to work that hard, and the autumn sun is low in the sky, covering everything it reaches in a golden wash.

This morning's events have left me emotionally drained but with a feeling of freedom and liberation that works well with being out of doors and travelling under my own steam.

Physical activity is an important part of my daily life. In fact, I would say it's crucial. Whether it's swimming, cycling, walking, or running, they all feed into my feeling of self-worth, and remind me what a gift it is to be alive, right now, in this moment. On a good day, like today, the combination of repetitive smooth muscle movement, cool fresh air in my lungs and an ever-changing landscape results in a kind of meditative feeling. It's at these times that I get to mull over things that are bothering me, seeing them with clarity, and from a more manageable perspective. This is a time to explore problems and look for possible solutions. I can think creatively without my inbuilt insecurities pushing through and knocking my confidence. The inner voices that tend to tell me I am rubbish, and laugh at my ideas, can't keep pace with my pedaling legs and racing mind.

Right now, I am cruising with a steady rhythm. My body is working efficiently, and I feel relaxed. My mind is released from the intensity of earlier on, and I have the space to reflect and process.

As I pedal, my thoughts focus on our recent experiences. We had known for the past six months that our friends were coming to stay. From day one, Mum had really struggled with this idea, and she was clearly very nervous about having guests. Looking back, I think it's plain to see that, at that time, she was more aware of her vulnerability than we were. We thought her worries about feeding and entertaining them were natural but over the top; we just didn't understand how she was feeling or recognise the seriousness of the situation.

The truth was that, to her, this visit represented an unpredictable and high-risk event that was loaded with unachievable responsibilities, each of which came with the possibility of being exposed, judged, and maybe ridiculed. This visit was a metaphorical minefield that, in my mum's view, did not need to be crossed. I must point out that these concerns are no reflection of the people who were coming to visit – they were more an indication of how my mum was feeling at that time. But sadly, we didn't listen to her concerns...or maybe we did listen but did not really hear what she was saying or recognise that she was fearful.

At that time Simon, Dad, and I were in a place where we were aware of her condition, but it was very much in the early stages, and we hadn't really anticipated the effect it could have on all our daily lives when faced with anything that was out of the ordinary. We had adjusted to repetitive behaviours and short-term memory issues, and we were doing a pretty good job of maintaining a positive and valuing environment for her. But we had totally underestimated the impact that announcing this visit would have on her wellbeing. So, we brushed her concerns to one side and continued to plan the details, naively assuming this would help her calm down and overcome the issues that were worrying her.

We were wrong.

As time moved on, and the arrival date edged closer, Mum's levels of anxiety escalated, and she was now showing very clear signs of stress. She was like a rabbit in the headlights, and unfortunately this experience also seemed to be exacerbating her symptoms of dementia. But by the time we realised this, the arrival date was so close that we felt there was very little we could do. Could we really back out at such short notice? Call the whole thing off? That didn't seem feasible – we just had to forge ahead with the plan and get through it.

This was a particularly tough time, especially for my dad who just wanted to do the right thing for everybody concerned. We spoke regularly on the phone, and as touchdown grew closer, to ensure his wife's concerns did not come to fruition, he had planned for every day and for every eventuality he could think of.

* * *

Having cycled a good distance, much farther than I intended, I do a U-turn and head back the way I came. What felt like a gentle tailwind on my outward journey now feels like a pretty harsh headwind. I drop down a gear or two and increase the cadence of my pedaling. This extra exertion brings me back to the job in hand with a jolt. It's hard work cycling into a coastal headwind.

Whenever I visit my parents and bring my bike with me, I always go out for a ride and, invariably, get lost on the way back, and today is no exception. What makes this particularly frustrating is that 90% of my ride is along the seafront, so there are limited opportunities to lose my way. If the sea is on my left, surely, I can't get lost? But as soon as I head inland for the last few miles, I become confused and take at least one wrong turn. The problem is that everything looks familiar. I have passed these trees and buildings on numerous occasions heading in all directions, but their rough location in relation to each other and my destination is a mystery. It would be helpful if I could connect each significant marker to the next, in some sort of logical sequence; then at least I would have an idea that I'm on the right road and heading in the right direction.

I wonder if this feeling of being lost despite being surrounded by familiarity is something my mum experiences as her illness progresses.

Eventually I spot a road sign saying *To the Seafront!* I follow it, retracing my route, hoping to get my bearings. I try again and eventually I spot the bingo hall, which tells me I am on the right track, and then in the distance I see a landmark, *"Our Windmill."*

I arrive home, and Mum laughs at me for getting lost. She tells me that if she still had the *sit up and beg* bike from her childhood, she could have come with me and shown me the way home. She would have enjoyed that.

* * *

Later that night, I am lying on my bed, in my old room, surrounded by all that stuff I didn't take when I left home but my parents don't feel they can throw away. I'm thinking again about our recent experiences.

So, what happened? How did the visit pan out?

Well, after months of nervous anticipation, our friends eventually arrived. Mum was welcoming, caring, and between them, she and Dad became the perfect hosts. Mum couldn't be happier to see them, and there was nothing she wouldn't do to ensure they had a great time. Dad had booked almost every meal at a restaurant, so the worry of food was mostly removed, which I must say was a master stroke. After all, we all know what it's like having people coming to stay when we are expected to feed them; anything over one or two days is a complete nightmare for most of us. But imagine, for a moment, having to deal with that when you are struggling to make sense of what's going on, you are not sure who people are, and you are in the dark and unconfident in relation to what is expected of you.

During the visit, the foursome went on trips to London, visiting Buckingham Palace, Saint Paul's Cathedral, and Westminster Abbey, where my mum enjoyed impressing everyone with her knowledge of the capital, World War II and the royal family. My dad heroically organised all of this, which is no mean feat.

Half-way through, I travelled up to Essex with the intention of helping out but, on reflection, I probably added to the pressure. Soon after I arrived, we went out for something to eat. It had been a very long time since I had seen our friends, and they were keen to talk about everything they had done since arriving in the UK. They were clearly having a great time, and this was mainly due to my lovely mum and dad doing all they could to ensure this was the case. It was during this conversation that I first became aware that Mum seemed to have completely blanked out, or lost, the last six months, and she now genuinely believed our visitors had just turned up unannounced. On several occasions, she even said this in front of them, and I am forever grateful that they never challenged or corrected her version of events. There appeared to be an unspoken agreement that the surprise visit was now everyone's truth. Our conversation on the journey back from the airport earlier today is proof enough that this is the story we will all live by – unless Mum changes the details, of course!

It's been a long day, and I'm totally shattered. I turn over in bed, and before going to sleep I reflect on what we have learned from this whole experience.

Well, the first point is that from this moment on we must really listen to what Mum says, take in her concerns, explore her support needs and then, together, plan what is and is not going to be happening. The second point is that although on the face of it the actual visit was a great success, this positive outcome was far overshadowed by the profound effect those months of anxiety and worry had on Mum's present and perhaps long-term wellbeing.

We did what we thought was right at the time, but looking forward it's vital that we reflect and learn from our mistakes as well as our successes.

Where the Magic Happens

Experience has taught me that when supporting somebody who is living with dementia, the more you know about them the better. This information helps you understand the wider context of their reality, enabling you to make connections and be with them in the moment. Of course, as in my case, you may already know them well, and you may be a part of their wider story. But if not, then it's important to take some time to find out as much as you can.

Look out for common ground and experiences which give you hooks into building a relationship. It's a solid starting point. Notice what makes them tick, what makes them laugh, what gives them a sense of pride, and what skills and knowledge they could share. While you are at it, take note of what kind of conversations they enjoy having, or, as in my mum's case, what stories they like to tell. For example, I guarantee that if you met her for the first time and you mentioned that you liked Johnny Mathis, you would instantly have a friend for life...or at least for the duration of the conversation! Find out what music makes them happy and what food and drink they enjoy the most. All this information will help the two of you to connect – and the value of two-way connections, even for a short or fleeting time, cannot be underestimated. This is where the magic happens, and the magic is priceless.

With this in mind, before I continue and you become more acquainted with my family and our experience of living with my mum's dementia, it is important that you also get to know her a little more by becoming familiar with her backstory. This will help you make sense of what she is saying and why, as well as what is important to her, and why she responds to certain situations in particular ways.

* * *

We all have our stories, and the following stories are significant because they are the ones my mum tells. She uses them to confirm her identity, her place in our family, in the community, and even in history. She also uses them to entertain and, at times, impress people or make them laugh.

But memory is fickle – this is her truth, as she sees it, and as she tells it. Like all stories from the past that are shared and retold, these have grown and flexed over the years, developing new connections and directions, sending out shoots and roots that attach themselves to the timeline of her life as she remembers it at any given moment.

Considering this, and out of respect for my wonderful mother, you the reader must go with her on this journey through her life without questioning dates, details or connections. You need to be, as we her family and loved ones are, with her in the moment.

One more point: While writing this book I have discovered that my memories too are fickle. My version of the truth may also differ from other people's and is no more, or less, valuable. All we can do is speak our personal truth and respect each other for doing so.

Part Two

Looking Back to Move Forwards

Upstairs Downstairs

Irene Edwina Meeks was born in Hertfordshire on the 9th of September 1932. She grew up in the bottom half of a big rambling house, in Parker Avenue, Bengeo, where she lived with her elder sister Sylvia, and their parents Ted and Flo. The couple did not own their accommodation. It came with their jobs as they were both in service for a well-to-do family, who lived in the top half of the house. It was all very *Upstairs Downstairs*, and their employers were known as *The Family*.

Ted and Flo had met in service in London. He was a driver, and she was a maid and cook. Their friendship turned to romance, and eventually Ted got down on one knee and proposed. Eager, but not wanting to be a complete pushover, Flo gave it a painful twenty-four hours of thought before accepting. Not long after marrying, the young couple decided to leave the capital and move to Hertfordshire to be closer to their families. They secured similar positions at 1 Parker Avenue, which came with good living quarters and the use of a small plot in the corner of a large garden. This meant they could start a family of their own. Their first daughter, Rose, tragically died within days of her birth. However, despite this devastating loss, they were soon to produce two more daughters, first Sylvia and then, within a year, Irene (Renee). Ted and Flo's employers were very supportive of the young family and made sure they were able to fulfil their roles in the busy household while also caring for two very young children. It was hard work and long hours, but they were happy with their lot and overjoyed with their two girls.

* * *

The car Ted chauffeured was kept in a lock up garage beneath the house, which was accessed via a narrow creaking staircase that led down from the kitchen. This closeness of proximity resulted in a unique cocktail of aromas. At the top of the stairs Flo would be cooking, baking pies, boiling sheets, and drying clothes for *The Family*. Meanwhile twelve steps below, Ted was creating a metallic oily smell mixed with tobacco, as he tinkered with the car engine and polished its chrome while smoking his pipe. According to Renee, this combination of smells was the "fragrance of home and family," and was at its most potent about halfway down the stairs.

Although the house was very grand with lots of places to play, run and hide (below stairs of course), it could also be a bit frightening for the girls. What with dark panelled walls that concealed mystery doors, heavy velvet curtains that provided ample room for strangers to hide, and the stairs that creaked and sighed even when nobody was climbing them, it was, understandably, quite easy to get spooked. Renee remembered numerous occasions when she and her sister would scare themselves by hiding in a place that seemed a good idea at the time, but a slight waft of air or a loose thread that felt like a cobweb would send them running, screaming and laughing into Flo's kitchen. Then they would be told to *hush*, reminded that *The Family* were living upstairs, and given useful jobs to keep them out of mischief.

Even the bright and colourful garden at the back of the house was edged with sinister-looking poplar trees, behind which was a dark and overgrown wood. Although they weren't supposed to go into the woods, the sisters would often squeeze through a low gap in the hedge and sneak about in the undergrowth. This was a place of fun and adventure, where they played games, built camps, and Renee, being more adventurous than her sister, would climb trees. But just like the house, the woods could easily play tricks on the girls' imagination and become a dark forest full of monsters and ghosts. This usually resulted in camps being abandoned and the two girls scuttling home at top speed, catching their breath and washing their knees before they were spotted by their mum.

However, despite the potential spooks and threats lurking in and around 1 Parker Avenue, Renee and Sylvia were very happy living there and created good memories of family life.

* * *

Flo had a strong faith, and despite the pressures of balancing upstairs and downstairs responsibilities, she always ensured prayers were said before meals and, crucially, the girls went to church on Sunday. And it was here, in Holy Trinity Church Bengeo, that young Renee first found her own, understated but ever-present, faith. She loved the familiar stories from the Bible, the clothes and regalia, the singing, and even the smell of the church. Occasionally the service would be held by a visiting clergy, and it was these visits that gave her the impression that she was now a part of something much bigger and more important than her daily life, and this provided a strong sense of belonging and safety.

In time she grew to know and understand the various celebrations in the Christian calendar and their associated themes and rituals. Being a great lover of words and stories, she soon memorised her favourite hymns, prayers, and carols, which she relished singing along with. But, as well as enjoying the experience of being part of the congregation, Renee was also a great listener, so began to understand the message and deeper meaning that was being conveyed, and it was this knowledge that formed the solid foundations of her lifelong beliefs.

* * *

When housekeeping allowed, Flo cooked a roast dinner with brown sugar-covered Yorkshire puddings on a Sunday, and then she would stretch out any leftover cold cuts and scraps to last through Monday and Tuesday and maybe become a bone broth on Wednesday or Thursday. She was born thrifty and was keen to pass this on, so she brought up her daughters to understand the importance of not wasting money, food, or clothes. She also taught them how to cook, wash, mend and keep house. From an early age Flo tried to instil in her daughters her view that the role of a woman in the household was bringing up the children, putting food on the table, and keeping the house and family presentable – all within the housekeeping allowance, while the man of the house, in this case her husband Ted, should go out to work and earn a living to support the family. This view of a woman's role was more a reflection of the times than anything intentionally limiting imposed by Ted. It was just the way things were back then in 1 Parker Avenue. This being said, Flo was also a fiery, opinionated character with a strong sense of what was right and wrong. She was very much in charge of the household and her family, she made the decisions and got the last word, so in short, Ted and the girls did what they were told. As Renee would often say, "It was *definitely* Flo who wore the trousers in that household!"

Ted, on the other hand, was a quiet, bespectacled man who loved horses and growing vegetables. When his career in service started in London, he was a stableboy and groom, eventually progressing on to become head groom. His role, at that time, was to oversee the care and tacking up of the horses, and to drive the carriages of his employers. But over the years, times changed. People began to prefer motor cars as their mode of transport and, because of this, to stay employed, grooms had to become chauffeurs. This meant that Ted, along with many of his peers from across the country, needed to learn to drive a motor car as soon as possible, which was a risky business as, being pre-1935, no driving tests were required! As well as learning to drive, he also needed to familiarise himself with car mechanics, as servicing and upkeep was all part of the job. Being a man with a natural and curious understanding of mechanics, and a built-in need for everything to be spotlessly clean, these new and additional responsibilities suited him very well, and he transitioned from horse to motor car very easily.

With transport becoming more comfortable, reliable, and faster, people got around a lot more and travelled further afield. This meant Ted got to know lots of people in service across London and the Home Counties. This growing network of friends came with benefits, including hot cups of tea by warm stoves, small talk, opportunities for swapping goods, and even meeting people of the opposite sex, and it was this last point that resulted in the blossoming romance and eventual marriage between Ted and Flo.

Like his wife, Ted was always well turned out, either in his work uniform, or trousers, braces, shirt, and tie. As well as keeping the car shining, he was also a very enthusiastic shoe polisher. What with this and Flo's near obsession with keeping the household brass and silver gleaming, the sound of vigorous polishing was a part of the soundtrack to life in Parker Avenue.

Renee idolised her dad. She loved his uniform and the fact that, in the days before most people had a car, he would chauffeur *The Family* around in a Rolls Royce. Now and again, if he was running an errand nearby, he would even collect the girls from school. When this happened, their teacher would call out in a high and excited voice, "Irene, Sylvia, your father is here to collect you!" Apparently, the very sight of her dad, smart and handsome in his chauffeur's hat, set the teacher's heart fluttering. According to Renee, his impeccable manners and apparent shyness added to the attraction.

Ted represented glamour, adventure, and freedom to his youngest daughter. "He would disappear in that car, to all sorts of exciting places with interesting people." She was in awe of this "other kind of life" that her dad had access to, and the fact that he was very discreet and even secretive about his work made it even more enchanting and mysterious.

* * *

Like for many of us, Renee's first real taste of independent freedom came when she learned to ride a bicycle. She pedaled up and down Parker Avenue with her dad holding onto the seat while she gained confidence, and then eventually, he let go and she felt like she was "flying as free as a bird." Her bicycle was what she described as a "sit up and beg bike with a basket on the front and a low crossbar." Initially it was too big for her, so there were some beginner's wobbles, and that first *flight like a bird* came to a swift halt when she crashed into a hedge. However, now she had tasted that wonderful sense of physical freedom, she wasn't going to let a few scrapes and bruises get the better of her, so she got back on her bike and kept trying, each time remaining upright for a little longer.

Whenever she fell off and came into the kitchen with scraped knees and elbows, Flo tried to put a stop to her antics, telling her "Bikes are for boys not girls!" But by this time, young Renee was already developing her lifelong aversion to being told what she could and couldn't do, so this potential restriction just made her more determined.

Once she had developed her confidence on two wheels, and Flo had given up on her campaign for keeping both feet firmly on the ground, Renee and her friend Ken would pedal off together down to the park in Hertford where they met their school friends on the swings and slide or sat by the river catching sticklebacks and crayfish with a net. Luckily, her sister was happy to stay home and enjoyed helping her mum with the housework. This conveniently enabled her to avoid some of the girls' chores and ride off looking for adventure, and it was at this time that she also developed her life-long love of wildlife and nature.

Two Bombs and One Crater

A week before Renee's seventh birthday, Great Britain declared war on Germany and World War II began. As with many households across the nation, this had an immediate and profound effect on life at 1 Parker Avenue. Windows were taped and blacked out, food was soon being rationed, and the cupboard under the stairs became the family air raid shelter.

With the onset of war, the local area also went through massive changes. As well as being conveniently just north of the capital, Hertfordshire was crucial to aircraft manufacture, with De Havilland designing and constructing their Mosquito and Halifax Bombers at the Hatfield Aerodrome. As a result of this, barracks were built in Hertford just down the hill from Bengeo, and the town soon filled up with soldiers, pilots, and, as the war progressed, American servicemen, and German prisoners of war (POWs). This influx of people to the local area was extremely exciting to the youngsters and, although they weren't supposed to be going into town on their bikes, Renee and her friends went on many secret missions to wave at the Americans and POWs. The days of catching sticklebacks and crayfish were already becoming a distant memory of a quieter time. This was an era of growing up quickly and enjoying American chocolate.

Seeing, and eventually speaking to, these people from far-flung places increased Renee's interest in other people and how they lived their lives. Americans were the most exotic of all. It seemed incredible to her that those handsome young men who had travelled all the way from America, a place that until now only existed in the cinema, were now an everyday sight in Hertford, and they were here to help her and her friends beat Hitler!

As well as the Americans, the spectacle of German POWs peering out from the back of canvas-covered lorries made an indelible impression on the youngsters. The first time they saw them, Renee went home and said to her mum, "They're people just like us, with mums, dads, brothers and sisters."

* * *

As the conflict continued, Ted was redeployed to become a civilian driver. His new role primarily involved transporting pilots and soldiers to and from training centres, barracks, and airfields in the area. Much to his daughter's delight, this new "military post" came with yet another fantastic uniform. Renee loved to see her dad heading out of the door, immaculate in his peaked cap. She saw him as an important part of the war effort. In her eyes he was a hero, and she was very proud of him. During this time Ted established a strong and long-lasting friendship with John 'Cat's Eyes' Cunningham, a very successful pilot throughout the Blitz, made even more famous by the press who gave him his nickname.

This change of job meant that the young family moved into rented accommodation, a small two-bedroom terraced house in Duncom Road, not far from Parker Avenue, but, as Renee said, "This move did make the war feel *real*."

* * *

Hertfordshire took its fair share of attacks from enemy aircraft, with approximately 4,000 bombs, 107 V-1 flying bombs, and 47 V-2 rockets falling on the county throughout the war.

Renee remembered, "It was frightening but also, in a strange way, exciting. The sirens were very loud, and the engines of the German bombers roared as they flew overhead on their way to London."

As soon as the air raid siren sounded, the girls would head for the now much smaller cupboard under the stairs, quickly grabbing their dolls and teddies on the way to make sure they were also kept safe.

Inevitably, due to the hours spent huddled in small spaces while just outside bombers growled and the world shuddered with fear, families developed strong and powerful bonds, and this was no different for Ted and Flo's young family. In this environment everything was stripped back to basics; this was about survival, belonging, and love. It was about people, not buildings.

There were two very significant bombs dropped in Renee's war, the first of which became a family legend and a much-repeated story. On this occasion, the air raid siren had sounded for the second time in an hour. This usually meant that the planes were on their way back from bombing London, so this was a slightly more worrying time as there was always a chance that any leftovers would be dropped on Hertford and the surrounding area. Flo and the girls were already in the shelter, and when Ted arrived home, he joined them. Although it was frightening, this kind of thing was also routine, so as usual Flo and Ted did all they could to reassure the girls that they were all safe, and they settled down and waited for the all-clear to sound.

But suddenly a heart-stopping, deep thud travelled right through their bodies, then a chorus of ear-piercing whistles, pops, and explosions. The ground shook, and the whole house seemed to groan and shudder. The small cupboard instantly filled with the sound of smashing glass and crockery. Then thick black dust dropped through the stairs and floorboards, making it difficult to breathe and almost impossible to see. The girls were coughing and covering their eyes, but it all happened so quickly they didn't have time to scream or cry.

Suddenly the noise and chaos stopped, and the house was enveloped by a deafening silence. Overwhelmed by what had happened, Flo became panicked and was convinced the house was gone. Her feeling of terror soon spread to the girls, who were not used to seeing such raw emotions from their mother.

After a few minutes of nervous tension, Ted, fully expecting to see piles of rubble underneath the dark night sky, slowly and tentatively pulled back the small brass catch and opened the door. However, to his great shock and relief, things appeared to be relatively sound, and what he saw was a dust-filled tiny lounge, a smashed window and soot falling out of the fireplace. The house had survived and he, his wife, and their daughters were spared.

Years later, whenever she described this scene, Renee said, "That bomb served to teach us what and who was important in life."

Once the dust had literally settled, Ted headed out into the night looking for damage and to offer refuge to anybody who had found themselves homeless or in need. It was a dark night, and it was mayhem as people tried to locate missing loved ones, pets, and belongings, or rushed to put out fires and care for the injured. In the true sense of community, cups of tea and blankets were soon handed out, followed by offers of help to people who had been worst hit. As Ted and his friends patrolled the streets, looking for any unexploded bombs and helping those that they could, they saw a great deal of destruction. Some houses and buildings seemed to have disappeared completely, and there were cracks and holes in the roads and pavements. Ted later remembered he had seen a tree that was smoking, but there were no flames or signs of fire. He said it was eerie because the tree was still covered in leaves, and the grass around its base looked unharmed. For some reason this was the clear memory that he took away from this terrible experience, and this was the story he chose to tell his two girls. Maybe the mysterious survival of the smoking tree was just easier to contemplate than the wider horror of what had taken place.

Although there was some damage close to home, Ted was baffled that he found no evidence of the bomb that felt like it had landed directly on their house. However, it was almost morning, he had been out all night, and things were as settled as they were going to be, so he said goodnight to his mates and made his way back to his family.

It was at this point he bumped into a neighbour, a member of the home guard, who congratulated him on his narrow escape. Seeing the quizzical look on his face, he added, "You had better head home, Ted; a bomb fell in your back garden, and your shed and vegetable patch have gone!"

On hearing this, Ted rushed home to find Flo, the girls, and a neighbour standing in the early morning light, peering down into a hole excitedly as if somebody, preferably a German pilot, was going to climb out of it. For some strange reason Renee and Sylvia were very proud of their bomb crater, they were so convinced of its *special*, even magical significance that they managed to charge a few people to come and see it. As bomb craters were a common sight during the war, I can't imagine they raised much money, but I do know the proceeds were donated to Mrs. Churchill's spitfire fund.

This story of my grandad, heading out into the night in search of a bomb that was in his back garden, has been told regularly throughout my mum's life. Her delivery is hilarious, full of laughter and pride. She is not only proud to have "dodged Hitler," but also proud of her family for being so brave and stoic in the face of real danger. Unfortunately, poor Ted had to bear the brunt of much banter and ridicule from his mates for many years to come.

The second significant bomb was, unfortunately, a direct hit on the girl's school, destroying buildings and shattering windows. Thankfully, this happened on a Sunday, so no children or teachers were killed or injured, but the school had to be closed for a few days while it was made safe.

Once it had reopened, lessons were held in the storerooms, outbuildings, and the dinner hall. This was all very exciting for the children, and the first day back was all about celebrating survival rather than fear of it happening again. It's interesting that, according to Mum, through the eyes of the youngsters, the act of going back into lessons was clearly linked to doing their bit towards winning the war. When I heard these stories, I wondered what the situation looked like through the eyes of parents and teachers. I would imagine it was far more threatening.

* * *

While Ted and Flo struggled to keep the family safe and fed, Flo's sister Auntie Kit was trying to do the same for other people's families. She lived in a village in the middle of Suffolk, and along the road from a farm where POWs were taken to work in the fields. Every morning, when their lorry passed through the village, it would stop outside her cottage and she would give them a bag of whatever food she could spare, such as fruit, bread and occasionally, if she could get hold of the ingredients, cake. This was impressive as, like everybody else, Auntie Kit lived on meagre rations. However, farming communities had more opportunities to trade local produce between themselves; this didn't make things any easier, but it did, at least, mean a slightly wider variety of foodstuffs were available. Once the food was handed over, Kit's little dog, Uno, would jump on board the lorry and they would drive out into the fields to start work. Uno was popular with the young prisoners and would do well from them sharing their food with him. Auntie Kit said she liked to look after the POWs because they all had mums who loved them, and she hoped that if her sons were ever in a similar situation they would be looked after too. After the war, Kit received a letter from one of the soldiers' mothers, thanking her for being so kind to her boy. When telling this story, Mum would remind us, once again, that "Everybody is loved by their mum and dad."

My dad had of course also experienced his war with his family and established similar strong bonds. Years later, this sense of connection and belonging was certainly something he and his wife worked hard to establish and nurture in our family.

Reading, Writing and Flirting

When she was eleven, Renee started attending Longmore School in Hertford. She enjoyed school life very much as it gave her a chance to do what she really loved doing – reading, writing, and spelling. She had taken to learning to read at an early age and took great pride in her abilities.

Occasionally, she would be asked to read in front of the class. Sometimes she was even asked to help other children who were struggling, encouraging them to break down longer words into syllables and then link them together to understand their meaning. The fact that the teacher singled her out to do this gave her a newfound confidence and belief that she actually had a talent, and she has carried this experience with her into adult life. Just this small gesture of positive feedback from a teacher significantly changed her view of herself, and her feelings of value to other people.

In her teenage years, Renee's enjoyment of reading led her to devour as many books as she could get her hands on. At weekends, when she wasn't with her friends, and her list of chores had been completed, she would cycle into town to sit in the library and read. She loved the classics, biographies, and the odd romance. Her ever-growing interest in the world around her, the world beyond Hertford, was now being explored through words and pictures. Much later she tried, successfully, to pass this passion for books onto me. I remember very clearly her buying me colourful hardback story books with fantastic pictures to enhance the experience and feed my imagination. She would get me to read these stories to her and to show her the pictures. *The Wind in the Willows* and *Pinocchio* were big favourites. Later, when I was in my teens, she borrowed library books for me to read. These were mostly novels she thought I'd like, some of which were more successful than others. *Oliver Twist* was a hit as was *Stig of the Dump*. However, *David Copperfield* and *Great Expectations* were dismissed as too heavy and boring and were not appreciated until about thirty years later.

Renee's interest in people's lives was not only fuelled by literature but also by films. She and her friend Rosemary became avid cinemagoers and would regularly attend the Saturday afternoon matinée, where they not only enjoyed the film but also took advantage of meeting, and sometimes flirting with, the local boys.

Renee Darlin'

By the time Renee reached the age of fourteen, the war was over, and she had secured a job as an office girl for the National Health Insurance Joint Committee, which in 1948 went on to become the National Health Service (NHS).

She loved her job and being in the thick of the action. Doctors and surgeons were frequent visitors to the office in Hertford, and like the boys at the cinema, they were great flirts with the office girls. This resulted in Renee answering to the name of *Renee Darlin'*. According to her, they were all "good-looking and had beautiful healing hands." Whenever she has mentioned this last detail in later life, Simon has always jumped straight in, trying to get details of any *hands-on shenanigans*. She laughs, but neither denies nor confirms the suggestion of an NHS romance.

She soon found her place in the office environment and was well respected by her employers and work friends. She put this down to her ability to spell and pronounce foreign names and medical terms. These skills put her in particularly good standing once the NHS was fully established, because a significant number of doctors and nurses came from overseas to work in the UK, and to be a part of this ground-breaking approach to healthcare for everybody. The people she met at work had a profound effect on her, and she truly believed that medical professionals were guided by a higher power to save lives and care for the sick.

Renee and her friend Rosemary were big football fans. Now they were earning money, they could get out and about. This would include getting up early on a Saturday morning and taking the green line bus to Highbury in London to watch their team Arsenal play. After the game, they would head off on foot into the city, walking to Oxford Street, Regent Street and Carnaby Street to look in the shop windows. They particularly enjoyed this during the festive season when Regent Street would be decorated with Christmas lights, and the big stores would put on fabulous window displays. In the summer months, the young women would walk along the embankment to visit parks, palaces, and cathedrals. St Paul's Cathedral and Westminster Abbey were firm favourites, and stepping into those massive buildings with towering spires and domes served to build on Renee's beliefs.

Cologne Cathedral

In her late teens, Renee had the opportunity to take her first trip abroad. Rosemary's dad was in the Royal Air Force and managed to take the two girls to Cologne in a military plane. The reason for this visit was never clear, but she remembered being driven around the city and seeing the undamaged cathedral standing alone, in what was still postwar devastation.

This wasn't newsreel at the cinema, photographs in a newspaper, or stories on the radio. It was a *real life* visit into a world that was inhabited by people who, for most of her young life, had been described as the enemy. But now, being present in this war-damaged city and witnessing the struggle and drive of ordinary people to rebuild their lives and homes made her think of the similar scenes she had seen in London with her dad the previous year.

On that day, as the bus wound its way through the suburbs heading towards the city, she saw areas of similar devastation, with people going about their day striving to create some kind of normality in which to move forwards and get on with their lives.

The people that really stood out for her in both London and Cologne were the children. They were playing, laughing, acting out imaginary adventures, and just being kids. There was no difference; they had just been born in different parts of the world, resulting in them being on different sides of a conflict they probably had very little understanding of, but that would continue to have a lasting effect throughout their lives.

Sitting next to her on the bus, Ted put his arm around his daughter's shoulder and said how lucky they were to have woken up that morning in their little house, had breakfast with her mum and sister and now here they were, the two of them sitting next to each other feeling safe and warm. He pointed out that lots of those kids playing on the streets of east London may have lost dads and brothers fighting overseas, or mums and sisters in air raids. The children they saw may have lost their homes and schools, but they were making the most of their situation and having fun.

Love and Marriage

As Renee and her friends approached their late teens, they started going out to dances and to see live music at the Hertford Corn Exchange. It was at one of these events that she met her future husband, Guy. The young couple were introduced by mutual friends named Joy and John. According to both, it was love at first sight, and it wasn't long before they were going out together on regular dates.

Guy lived in the village of Roydon, which sits on the border between Essex and Hertfordshire about nine miles from Bengeo, a short drive for him in his recently acquired Hillman Minx. Over time, the young couple's romance developed into a deep bond and devotion that continued to grow and strengthen throughout the years. They were, literally, the loves of each other's lives.

Guy was soon introduced to his future in-laws, who took to him quickly and treated him as the son they never had. Ted was particularly fond of him, and looked forward to his visits so they could go off to the pub together. This was a little frustrating for Renee, who seemed to be in competition with her dad for Guy's attention. However, the blossoming of the two men's friendship paid dividends when the time came for Guy to ask permission to marry Ted and Flo's youngest daughter.

In 1958, the young couple married in a registry office in Hertford. Guy, wearing a very nice-fitting Italian-style suit with a narrow tie. Renee in a white calf-length wedding dress that flared out from her narrow waist. In the photographs they look amazingly cool and sixties – even if it was still the fifties. Once back from their honeymoon in Eastbourne, they moved to Roydon and set up home in a small two-bedroom prefab bungalow with Crittall windows, and an electric heater hanging precariously over the enamel bathtub.

* * *

Guy was foreman of a grain drying business; the bungalow came with his job and was situated between giant redbrick warehouses, a tall concrete tower called The Dryer, some black Nissan Huts, and a thick-walled air raid shelter left over from the war. It was a strange environment for Renee to find herself in. Although their home was technically in the village, she and Guy had no close neighbours. Farmland and a graveyard stood between them and the rest of the community. This was a big change from life in Bengeo, where neighbours lived close together and, as a result of coming through the war together, had a very strong social bond.

Initially, she felt isolated from her family in this new and strange world, and for a while the only people, other than her husband, that she saw were workmen and farmers. However, being a woman who knew what she wanted, she decided she wasn't going to sit back and stew in her feelings of loneliness, so she proactively involved herself in village life, going to church, visiting the hairdressers, shopping in the village grocers, and of course getting to know her new in-laws.

Guy had two younger brothers named Reg and Pete, and their dad, Leonard, was the village policeman. His mum, Iris, kept house and liked half a Guinness when she could get one. Renee became close to the family and soon established herself as a central figure in gatherings, events and even the odd crises. The in-laws lived in the police house at the other end of the village, which was conveniently close enough to visit, but also a comfortable distance away from the young couple, enabling them to get on with their lives without too much interference. In time, Renee made some new acquaintances outside of the family, some of whom would turn out to be wonderful life-long friends.

Becoming Mum and Dad

Once they had settled into married life and their new home, Renee became pregnant with Martin, who was born in 1961 and then me – Marcus – born in 1964. Renee and Guy were now Mum and Dad.

My pre-school life revolved around my mum, who, by this time, had given up her much-loved job at the NHS to take care of us kids. Dad was out working long hours, and my brother, being three years older, was already at nursery or real school. Our bungalow had a tiny lounge with a small window that looked out over a raised flower bed towards the Nissan Huts, beyond which were farmed fields, streams, hills, and the woodlands of Essex. This landscape formed the backdrop to our family life.

The lounge had a small, orange furry rug in front of the fire. On cold days, me and Carny the Labrador would squeeze onto the rug together, as if it was a warm and comfy lifeboat set adrift in a sea of icy cold linoleum, which it kind of was. However, Carny did have a terrible flatulence problem so, occasionally, I had no choice but to bail out and take my chances on the wild and swirly lino.

In the corner of the room there was a small black and white television with two channels, on which we would watch my favourites: *Pogles' Wood* and *Noggin the Nog*. In these modern times of the internet, it is interesting to revisit some of these children's television shows from the sixties and to realise how weird and sinister they could be. There was always a dark force involved that threatened to ruin everything. I can't speak for anyone else, and I don't want to overemphasise the effect of Mr. and Mrs. Pogle, but I definitely bought into this idea of unknown but ever-present dark threats, and maybe I have kept it with me into adulthood.

* * *

Martin and I shared a small box room, with bunk beds and a *Noddy* wall light that buzzed, fizzed, and sparked whenever it was switched on. I was on the top bunk, which I got into by climbing a wooden ladder. Martin slept on the bottom bunk, just a few feet below me. Sometimes he would wait until I was all tucked up in bed and the lights were off, and then he would silently slip his hand up the side of my bed and suddenly grab me around the neck. I knew it was him, but this seemed to make little or no difference to my terror. Maybe, at that time, my version of the dark, threatening presence in *Pogles' Wood* was in fact an aggravating kid who slept on the bottom bunk!

This sudden strangulation trick was just one of many hilarious strategies Martin used to keep me whining and whinging. Whenever he pulled one of his pranks, I would bolt down the ladder headfirst, run out of the room and, sobbing, jump into Mum and Dad's bed. It must have driven them mad. I was a very needy little kid, which resulted in me regularly crawling into their bed for one reason or another. Usually after a calming few minutes, I would be coaxed into returning to the top bunk with my mum whispering in my ear the familiar, "Night, night, sleep tight, and remember...don't let the bed bugs bite!"

Looking back, I now realise that my visits to my poor mum and dad probably contributed to our little family never growing any bigger.

* * *

At this time Mum was working from home sewing the seams of leather motorbike goggles. This was known as *Goggling.* I remember her sitting in her chair telling me stories and fairy tales as she pushed the thick needle and thread through the leather goggles, using a steel thimble to apply extra pressure. I can still smell the soft, pliable leather whenever I think about it.

At other times we would do things together like colouring in pictures, or my favourite activity, knitting scarfs! I was a prolific pre-school knitter. My mum taught me at a very early age, and every Christmas I would get a knitting kit as a present. I loved it, and although my repertoire was limited, with her help I did, over the years, manage to provide the extended family with individualised scarves, some with attached woolly balls or tassels, but all with holes and uneven edges. I really thought I'd found my place in the world with my knitting, and the truth is I would probably still be cranking up the needles if it hadn't been for a family-wide practical joke that backfired horrendously, causing me huge humiliation at a very early age and resulting in me casting off and putting away my needles for the very last time.

Despite this incident, those pre-school days were cosy, warm, and snug, and it was at this time that my mum and I really established a close bond and understanding. Of course, this is natural between a parent and a child, but what I would say is that I think she noticed in me issues of confidence. I felt like I was on the outside looking in, and I think even at that young age I recognised similar characteristics in her. We were kindred spirits and have continued to be so ever since.

* * *

Once us two boys were both settled into school life, Mum decided to go back to work for the NHS. However, with the office being ten miles from her new home, and with no direct train or bus to Hertford, she needed to find a way of getting there, so she set about learning to drive. My dad, always the hero, took on the task of teaching her. I can't imagine what the atmosphere was like in the car, because the woman I know and love is not a natural when it comes to being told what to do, especially by her husband. Maybe their marriage was still in the *Honeymoon Period*, and it was all love and butterflies. Anyway, whatever the atmosphere, the lessons were a great success, and much to everyone's surprise, including her own, Mum passed her driving test first time. She was the first of her female friends to start driving and was very proud of what she had achieved. This is just one of the many stories Mum likes to tell, and she really went to town much later when I failed my driving test for the first and second time. I'm not sure if that really helped me feel better, but *she* certainly enjoyed the glory.

Following this success, Mum went straight out and bought a little blue and cream Mini, which she drove to her office in Hertford every day. She was married, had set up home, and had two kids at school. *Renee Darlin'* was all grown up!

Village People

Roydon was a small village with a train line directly into London. It had a short high street with a butcher, a post office, a doctor's surgery, an all-important hairdresser, and, even more important, four pubs. It was a very social place where people knew each other, and most people frequented at least one of the pubs regularly. Mum and Dad's local was The New Inn, with a low, beamed ceiling, well-used ashtrays, pewter tankards, and a beer garden. The publicans, Reg and Eileen, sat at the centre of a strong community of social drinkers, who were up for a laugh and attached great importance to Friday and Saturday nights in the pub.

When Martin and I were too young to drink (even by 1970s standards), my nan (Flo) would come and stay at the bungalow and babysit to allow Mum and Dad to go out and let their hair down. As we got a little older, we were left at home by ourselves. Martin, being the eldest, was the nominated babysitter – I think this may have been an early experiment in positive risk-taking, and I wouldn't say it was a great success. On several occasions, the risks far outweighed the benefits, and the evening would end in fights and tears. Usually, Martin would come out on top, but there was one memorable evening when I clumped him around the head with a broom handle and, for a short while, knocked him out. My memory of this event is that it was the catalyst for me and my brother to recalibrate our relationship – to one of mutual respect shrouded by avoidance and complete disdain.

When we were in our early to mid-teens, we would go to the pub ourselves, first drinking coke, then quickly graduating to shandy, and sneaky beers. Underage drinking was the norm back then, as was drinking and driving. If you were the nominated driver, it just meant that you weren't quite as drunk as your passengers.

Occasionally, what felt like half the village descended on our bungalow for an impromptu post-pub party. Dad would put his *Top of the Pops* LP on the hi-fi system, and Mum would knock up a cheese, potato, and onion pie. The men would drink beer from a giant *Party Seven* can, while the women drank Cinzano or Martini. These parties and lock-ins at the pub became legendary, with all sorts of associated tales and myths which, every now and again, still make an appearance in our conversations.

Throughout this time, Mum and Dad, along with their friends, regularly went to London to attend concerts by the likes of Frank Sinatra, Tony Bennett and, of course, Johnny Mathis. They always managed to get good seats close to the front (enabling Mr. Mathis to speak directly to my mum of course), and they usually went out for a meal afterwards to round off the evening with a steak and a few drinks.

These events were eagerly anticipated and the highlight of the calendar year. Mum, who was always on a diet, really upped the stakes and lived on grapefruit and cottage cheese for months on end, all to lose a few pounds for the star of the evening.

One of the many diets she went on involved regular visits to the doctor. This particular weight loss plan really worked, the pounds dropped off and Mum was buzzing – literally buzzing. It turned out this specific diet involved regularly taking amphetamines (Speed). Mum was losing weight; the house was spotless, and poor old Carny the farting Labrador was almost walked to death. The diet didn't last long because you were only allowed to take the drug for six weeks – otherwise you were at risk of becoming an addict, so Mum would have had to go cold turkey.

She didn't need to lose weight as she had a great figure, but my memory tells me that whenever they hit the town and attended these concerts, she always looked spectacular – so job done.

Polk Street and Leather Boys

Once we had left school, both Martin and I started to find our own lives and eventually left home. Against all odds, Martin found himself living in California for twenty-two years. He married, had a child and, tragically, lost his wife far too young. I spent about fourteen years moving around from country to country, seeing the world and trying to find out who I was. This meant that for a significant amount of time I saw very little of Mum and Dad, and Martin even less so. Over those years there were times when our paths did cross, or at least 75% did – that was when either me or Martin came home to the UK for one reason or another, but as a family, the full 100% was a very rare occurrence.

Probably the most memorable time that we did all get together was in California in the late 1980s. I was living and working in San Francisco as a bike messenger, and Martin, having found his calling as a skilled carpenter, was working and living with his American family in a place called Placerville. Having not yet met Martin's wife or baby, Mum and Dad decided to come and visit, so we all met up for a few days in San Francisco. This was a crazy experience on so many levels.

Although I had been living in the city for about eighteen months by this point, I hadn't really thought about what it would be like if my parents ever came to stay. I lived with my friend Niki, in a room on the fifth floor of one of those cheap residential hotels that are, or at least were, a feature of most cities in the U.S. The Leland Hotel was populated by a mainly permanent collection of fabulous, interesting, and diverse residents. These included drag queens, transsexuals, leather boys, and lots of gay men. There were also a few very exotic characters, including a man with a long beard who regularly wore a nun's habit, and an older woman who often went out dressed as a Roman Centurion. Perhaps most surprising of all, there was a fantastic community of very straight young men and women who seemed to enjoy the atmosphere of this weird and wonderful place.

Niki and I had ended up living at the Leland by accident. We had arrived at the Greyhound Bus Station, on Mission Street early one morning with nowhere to stay and spotted a card advertising cheap rooms pinned to the wall of a payphone. The hotel was situated on Polk Street, which, by its very nature and character, suited the clientele of the Leland very well. There were bars, cafés, stores and clubs, and the street corner below our window provided good passing trade for our new friends who made a living from their looks and bodies. So, it's fair to say that the general vibe was *anything goes* on Polk Street.

* * *

Being the mid-eighties, San Francisco, and particularly the gay community, was in the maelstrom of living through the AIDS crisis. In fact, *crisis* isn't a strong enough word to describe what was taking place. AIDS was an all-encompassing threat with so many unknowns, rumours and scare stories, that it was difficult to know how to stay safe. All that was known was that the virus was randomly and quickly taking people's lives and leaving a trail of devastation behind it.

On reflection, I think myself and Niki were naive as to the

impact this epidemic was actually having on the people around us. Although we lived in the centre of the community and had made lots of friends, due to our *foreignness* and our accents, we found ourselves slightly on the outside looking in. This sounds strange when I write it down, but it felt almost as if we were detached from reality. This perception of difference and separation came with risks, a kind of subconscious assumption of immunity. This, along with the natural immortality of youth, meant that I certainly made some unwise decisions at that time and put myself in jeopardy, telling myself that *being infected by viruses and dying is something that old people do, not healthy young ones.*

However, despite this dark cloud that hung over the city, San Francisco was still a very exciting, creative and energised place to be living, and for me, music played a major role in creating this atmosphere. Even now just hearing Grace Jones, "Pull Up to the Bumper," Madonna, "Open Your Heart," or George and Aretha, "I Knew You Were Waiting," can transport me back to sitting in our favourite bar, *The QT*, swigging cold Corona with a wedge of lime, and smoking Marlborough Lights. It also reminds me of watching the handsome and immortal young men, dancing, flirting, and having a great night...almost as if it may be their last.

I hope that they are still around, a bit older, but living their best lives.

* * *

The strange thing is that when Mum and Dad visited, rather than booking them into a nice hotel in the city, or on Fisherman's Wharf, I had booked them a room at the Leland, and it really wasn't until they arrived that I thought about the culture shock of going from rural village life in Essex to gay village life in San Francisco. What made it doubly strange was, at that point, I hadn't told my parents about my own sexuality. In fact, my memory tells me that I was proactively hiding it from them, although, on reflection, I must say I wasn't making a very good job of it.

Despite my lack of planning, the visit was a great success. We walked across the Golden Gate Bridge singing Tony Bennett songs; Mum got locked up in the same prison cell as Clint Eastwood in *Escape from Alcatraz*. We visited Lombard Street – *the crookedest street in the world*, and I drove us down Columbus Avenue, where *Bullet* with Steve McQueen was filmed. We also survived an earth tremor that woke us all in the night, rooms shaking and pictures swaying on their hooks. This left us shaken but not stirred.

As well as meeting Martin's new family, Mum and Dad also got to meet some of our new friends, whom Mum later spotted getting in and out of strangers' cars in the street below her window. I know this because one morning she whispered to me with a worldly look, "I know how Rory and Steve earn their money." I didn't respond, as this subject was a step too far in our mum and son relationship.

A little later, as my dad and I walked down Polk Street, with him wearing his pink and grey diamond Pringle jumper, he said to me – "I suppose people just assume I am paying for your company, do they?" Again, I chose to ignore this comment and block out any connotations!

And Life Continues...

The stories I have shared so far are significant because they, along with our musical soundtrack and cultural influences, have become a part of our family narrative, and form the rich fabric that holds us together, keeps us grounded, and reminds us who we are and what is important.

But of course our story doesn't end with me and my dad walking down Polk Street in the late eighties – it continues through until the present day.

New experiences, events, challenges and encounters mix and blend with those of the past and together they influence our responses, our memories and our individual versions of the truth. Out of this emerge new stories that keep us on our toes, entertained, and ensure we continue living together, in the moment.

So what else has happened in the meantime?

Well, Carny the Labrador of our childhood let out his final contribution to global warming before shuffling off the orange rug and making his way across the swirly lino. Over the years all our grandparents have also passed away – Flo, in control of the proceedings, made sure she was the last to go.

The bungalow, air raid shelters and Nissan Huts were all demolished and replaced with riverside houses – but not before Mum and Dad left Roydon and moved up to Clacton-on-Sea, where they found a new quieter, but no less enjoyable life.

I came back to the UK and eventually settled down on the south coast with Simon, a pug called Milo, and a green campervan. In time Martin returned from California and set up home with his partner Helen.

And life continues...

Part Three

Early Signs and Ostriches

As you have seen, my mum has led a remarkable life, full of love, laughs, heartache, and achievements. She has worked hard, raised kids, maintained a strong and loving marriage, and been a great friend to many. She has also gone through life putting herself very much at the centre of the action. If people are laughing, she can usually be found somewhere in the middle of the crowd, either telling one of her ever-evolving stories, of which there are many, or alternatively, adding witty comments or questions to other people's stories (this is an annoying habit I am proud to say I have inherited directly from her – minus the wit).

But at a certain point in her life, her mid-seventies, there were some subtle but clear changes in her behaviour and abilities. These changes weren't life-changing, but they were, nevertheless, out of character. Initially they were just occasional memory-related episodes. For example, struggling to put names to faces, remembering what day it was, or repeating what had just been said. Like I say, not life-changing, but noticeable.

Although I had my suspicions that these changes may have been indicative of a more serious problem, at that time I chose to see things from an objective point of view and resisted making any sweeping assumptions. I must say that I found this surprisingly easy to achieve, because I could totally relate to, and normalise, what was going on for her. I regularly have similar experiences myself. Depending on how strong my resilience is at any time, challenging events or issues can subtly influence my ability to fully function in an everyday social way. When this happens, I become a little detached and at odds with what is taking place in my immediate vicinity, and because of this I can struggle to recall information, recent conversations, or people's names.

For me, these episodes of mind fog can be triggered by either physiological problems, for example, being in pain or discomfort, or psychological issues, such as feeling overwhelmed, anxious, or upset about something. At these times, I can become so preoccupied that I am almost unaware, or don't really care about what's going on around me; I just don't have the space in my head to give anything else my attention. That sounds a bit dramatic, but I don't think I'm alone in this, am I?

Where my experience may differ from my mum's is that when it happens to me, I feel confident that in time the fog will clear and I will be back to firing on all, or at least most, cylinders. Whereas for her that reassurance and confidence did not appear to be there, and although the spells of confusion were short-lived, they seemed to feel open-ended, which of course was frightening for her and exacerbated the problem.

So, when we first noticed these changes, I emotionally distanced myself from what was happening and tried to view it from a rational perspective. I focused on the facts – what I saw, and what I knew. This was tough; how can you disconnect from emotions when you are thinking about your parent's wellbeing? I didn't talk about my concerns to anybody, as that would almost *out* it as an issue. Also, I was acutely aware that if I started to speak about it to my dad, it would cause him worry and anxiety, which was the last thing I wanted to do. So, I let it go, and like an ostrich, I stuck my head in the sand. Of course, with hindsight, it is obvious my dad, who was living with his wife seven days a week, was aware of the changes in her behaviour and abilities. He had, as it turned out, noticed them long before I did, and now I regret not having had a conversation with him earlier. I suppose I was in a place where I couldn't acknowledge my concerns to others until I had acknowledged them to myself.

But in addition to this, I was aware that the behaviours Mum was displaying could have been related to some other underlying issues, such as a urinary tract infection, some of the symptoms of which are similar or the same as those of dementia, so I kind of clung onto that idea for a while. Although this thinking was valid, logical, and required some further investigation, to be frank, there was also some self-preservation going on here. I was protecting myself and others from the possibility that her symptoms *were* related to dementia, and that was an idea that was too much for me to fully take on board at that point.

* * *

Eventually, of course, we were forced to openly discuss what was happening because what at first seemed like insignificant isolated incidents of confusion gradually occurred more and more often, until they became the norm rather than the exception. By this time, Simon, Dad, and I recognised and eventually acknowledged these memory issues were probably linked to dementia, and over the following months this probability was increased as Mum underwent various tests for infections and conditions, which were ruled out as a possible cause. However, with no dementia assessment, there was no diagnosis.

Having had previous experience of working with people living with dementia, I had some understanding of what this could mean, and what kind of support was required. Before the event, I thought that this experience and knowledge would help me cope with the possibility of somebody I loved developing the condition. However, the truth was that when it did happen, I was not prepared at all. I just couldn't apply any of my previous learning to this situation. If I'm being honest, I would say that I just couldn't take my own advice. After all, this was my mum, my fabulous mum, one of the two people who had been a constant source of strength and support to me throughout my whole life. But, despite how I was feeling, it was clear that I didn't have the luxury of keeping my head in the sand any longer, and I had to face the fact that this was real. It was happening now, and ignoring it was of no help to anybody.

At this point, it is fair to say that my previous experience, knowledge, skills, and confidence counted for nothing. My emotions and fear got the better of me, and, in private, my mind was filled with myths, horror stories and cliches. I knew these fears may not come to fruition, but it made no difference; I jumped to the worst-case scenario at every twist and turn and developed a huge internal list of *what ifs*.

So, what was on this list? What were my fears?

That Mum would be confused and frightened. That she would lose her sense of identity and her pride in who she was. That other people would judge her negatively. That she would become invisible and be avoided by people she loved or enjoyed talking to. I was fearful that she might need support with personal care, or that she might get to a point where she didn't know our names or who we were, or that just to communicate her emotions she may have to resort to behaviours that people would find challenging or aggressive. I was also scared that my dad would become isolated and heartbroken, and I wouldn't be able to support or rescue him. The list was endless and cast a dark and creeping shadow that was regularly present in some way for a considerable time.

I couldn't share what I was feeling with my dad as I needed to be there to support him and his wife. I wanted to be positive every step of the way, offering reassurance and solutions, but this could be a struggle depending on what was going on for me at the time. However, Simon has years of professional experience supporting people to live well with dementia. He manages a service that does just that, so he has a great deal of expertise in the illness, the impact it can have, and what practical steps can be taken to improve the situation. His pragmatic approach helped me, my dad, and the rest of our family step back a little from our worries, avoid inventing negative futures, and instead put our energy into the here and now – and what we *could* influence.

Deciding, whenever we feel able, to consciously adopt Simon's mindset is probably the best move we have made in relation to my mum's and our experience of her dementia.

Note to the reader – it turns out that ostriches do not stick their heads in the sand. That is a myth. However, when the going gets tough, I have proved to be adept at it.

Part Four

Living Well with Dementia

It's 2007, three years since the first signs of Mum's illness became apparent. Although there is a clear trajectory, thankfully, the decline in her abilities is surprisingly slow and is not linear. In fact, it seems to go through peaks, troughs, spirals, and occasionally, complete U-turns. Times of confusion are often followed by long periods of plateauing – *steady state* – with nothing any different happening. Then, unexpectedly, these periods are disrupted by invisible incidents or obvious events that trigger a significant change or reduction in her cognitive abilities. Following these episodes there is often some clawing back, but at other times the decline is more permanent and sets in for the long haul.

As we, her family and loved ones, become acquainted with these fluctuations and nuances, we proactively do all we can to manage them while striving to maintain a positive and empowering environment that enables us all to live well with her dementia. This may sound very much like we do this, *to* or *for* her, but that is not the case at all. The truth is that we are all in this *together*, and Renee Batterbury is clearly the driver. After all, she knows herself best, and she knows how she wants to live her life.

So, together, we take things one day at a time, learning from our mistakes as well as our successes. We keep one eye on the road ahead and swerve obstacles and triggers wherever possible. But, overall, we live very much in the moment with mutual respect, love, and a fair amount of humour.

At this point it is important to acknowledge that Mum's condition is just one element of our story. It does not define her or us. It is a crucially important and impactful element but, nonetheless, it is just one part of a bigger picture. The world hasn't stopped *because* of her illness – that would just give it the upper hand. The reality is that life continues, with all its ups, downs, triumphs, and tragedies – *despite* her illness. So, we have needed to broaden our scope of thinking and see the world through a wide-angle lens to make the very most of every experience and ensure we are living as best we can.

* * *

The following chapters are a continuation of our story – spanning from the early years of living with Mum's dementia, through to the present day. Together, these chapters not only explore our many challenges, successes, mistakes, and lessons learnt along the way, but also shine a light on the simple ideas that work for us, solutions we have stumbled upon, and techniques we have discovered that help Mum live as well as she can – most of the time.

But this story is not about a disease, it's about a family – and as we all know, families are very strange – and writing this book, I have realised that mine is no exception.

A Walk on the Wild Side

It's autumn of 2008, and something unexpected has happened. My parents went to a charity coffee morning around the corner from where they live – this is surprising because Dad just isn't a *coffee morning* kind of guy. But the fact that they went does show that they are not letting Mum's condition keep them from engaging with other people, so that's a good thing.

There were about twenty people present, all milling around chatting, buying drinks and cakes, and not really knowing what they were supposed to be doing. Meanwhile, the hosts were doing their best to raise more money by selling raffle tickets while fussing over the prizes. These included a large tin of chocolates, a bottle of wine, some gardening gloves, a fruit cake, and a few mystery envelopes.

Despite Dad's discomfort, and efforts to make a swift exit from his first and last coffee morning, he obediently bought a few tickets and they stayed until the end. Once the coffee cups were drained, the cake had been eaten, and the raffle was being called, to their mutual embarrassment they discovered they not only had a winning ticket, but they had won the first prize. On hearing this news, Dad's already wavering spirits sagged a little further as he contemplated gratefully accepting a trouser press or a set of matching oven gloves, but instead he was handed one of the mystery envelopes. *Good, it's a voucher*, he thought to himself with relief as he slipped it into his pocket and headed for the door. But their way was blocked, and the hosts insisted they open the envelope and discover the treasure within in front of everybody. This really was turning into a cringe-fest for my poor old dad. If he'd known they would win, he wouldn't have bought a ticket. But, giving in to pressure, he handed the envelope to Mum, who opened it and, after studying it for a few hesitant seconds, read out, "Congratulations, you have won a week's holiday in Cyprus!"

Initially he thought his wife had made an unlikely mistake. Yes, she was continuing to have challenges with her abilities, but up until now, her reading had continued to be spot on, and it would be a cruel twist of fate if she were to lose the ability she was the most proud of. Well, thankfully, that was not the case. Unbelievably, this tiny raffle, that at most can only have raised a couple of hundred quid for charity, had a top prize of a holiday for four in Cyprus! And it is this highly unlikely event that has resulted in Mum, Dad, Martin, and I sitting in the departures lounge of Stansted Airport waiting to board a plane heading southeast.

* * *

This morning was chaotic, funny, and stressful in equal measures. Simon was our chauffeur and drove us to the airport in Fanny the Campervan – to say it was a squeeze is an understatement. It was so cosy that Mum only narrowly escaped having to sit on Martin's lap. Luckily for both parties, I prevented this happening by spending the entire journey facing backwards perched on a box that wasn't attached to the van. As Simon tried to impress a captive but nervous audience with his recently acquired driving skills, I slid from side to side, facing Martin and then Mum alternately. While doing this I contemplated the realities of the little adventure we were about to set out on. Judging by the hint of apprehension on both of their faces, I wondered if they were having similar thoughts to me. To be honest, I felt a tad nervous – seven days together... alone. What on earth would we talk about? The strangeness of this event was only just sinking in. I felt all at sea about it, and my sliding from port to starboard as Fanny twisted and turned her way to the airport was just adding to this sensation, taking me almost to the point of sea sickness.

* * *

Later, having survived the flight, collected our luggage and been ripped off by a slightly sinister taxi driver, we have arrived in our apartment, which I am surprised to discover is in Ayia Napa. I've heard of this place, and in the back of my mind I am pretty sure that it is famous for hen-do's, stag-do's and naked foam parties... God help us.

The apartment is basic but clean, with a small outside courtyard, an open-plan lounge and kitchen, a bathroom and two bedrooms. This last detail means Martin and I will be sharing a room. Not sure how I feel about that, but I'm relieved to see there are two single beds, as opposed to bunk beds, as I really don't fancy climbing in with Mum and Dad, not at this point in my life...not in my late forties.

This all feels very strange – it is so rare that the four of us are alone together for any length of time; in fact I can't remember when it last happened, but it has definitely been decades...surely not Polk Street? Martin and I have already resorted to telling each other dirty stories, in hushed tones, which is quite entertaining and even educational, owing to the fact that we bat for opposite teams.

After settling in we go out for something to eat and, with the help of a few beers, we eventually begin to relax and reconnect. We talk about the past and catch up on what we have all been up to. It occurs to me that since Martin returned from the USA, he and I haven't really got round to having a normal conversation. In truth we don't really know each other. So much has happened in our lives since we last had a real chat. This is good. A little weird and slightly uncomfortable, but good.

One of the obvious things that has happened which has an impact on all of us to differing degrees is, of course, Mum's illness. But this isn't something we openly discuss, as she is not in a place where she is comfortable or, indeed, interested in acknowledging any possible problem. From her point of view, these incidents of confusion are individual, stand-alone episodes, and there is no need for speculation or the mention of restrictive and loaded labels such as *dementia.* I get that, I really do; it makes perfect sense. My mum is a woman who has avoided labels all her life, and I have inherited this from her, so I completely understand her reticence – as she once told me: "Labels are for jam jars, not people."

* * *

Almost four years have passed since Mum's symptoms started to become apparent, and according to my dad, other than the severe dip that was brought on by the well-intentioned visit from overseas, thankfully it's been mostly plain sailing. But being so close to the situation and focusing mainly on ensuring things are as good as they can be on a daily basis, he is curious to know how it looks from a slightly more distant perspective. He is unsure if her condition is noticeably progressing and about how she is feeling within herself. In addition to this, he is not certain if he is doing too much, or not enough, and what effect any of this might be having on his wife.

So, when we walk along the seafront, I walk with Mum. When we eat in restaurants and bars, I sit with her, and back at the apartment in the evenings I spend my time chatting to her. Initially, things do look pretty good. She appears to have a high sense of personal wellbeing, and I am reassured to realise that although her symptoms are very apparent, there doesn't seem to be any noticeable decline. However, I continue to keep an eye and ear out for anything I've missed up until now.

But after just two days of our holiday, I find it difficult to relax and enjoy the time we are spending together, and instead I am preoccupied. I am constantly looking for signs and evidence of something more sinister going on, and to add to this, my mum has made it very clear she recognises what I am doing, and she knows I am up to no good. She and I are very close, and it is completely normal for us to spend lots of time together, but she can sense my scrutiny, and because of this she has an air of suspicion about her. I know this because she has become subtly defensive and is overcompensating to scupper my enquiries about her abilities or struggles.

On reflection I realise that despite my best intentions, I am looking through a lens of negativity – and to what end? What am I trying to prove? What will be different as a result of this focused attention? I have a hidden agenda, which is disrespectful, and, on some level, Mum is aware of what I am doing. It is now clear that the rock-solid trust that our relationship has been built on has inadvertently taken a knock, and I don't know what to do about it, but I do know that I don't want to be that devious person. So, I do my best to shake myself out of it and just focus on the pleasure of being on holiday with my family, and particularly with my super intuitive mother, right now in the moment.

* * *

It's mid-week and I am swimming in the bay near our apartment. Mum, Dad, and Martin are sitting on the seafront. It's weird that although she lives with short-term memory loss and it is very likely she can't remember our experiences of earlier in the week, I am pretty convinced Mum does remember how I made her feel – the residual emotions are still with her, and as a result she is very slightly standoffish with me – nobody would notice this, but I do, and I am annoyed with myself for putting unnecessary pressure on her, and jeopardising our cherished relationship, even if only for a short time.

As I swim, I am convinced I am being observed by Martin. We have spent so little of our adult lives together that we both seem to have a curiosity about the other's skills and abilities. We have been getting on well, but maybe there is a subtle undercurrent of trying to get the measure of each other? Perhaps that natural childhood competitiveness has re-emerged?

Being a regular swimmer, I stepped into the water with an air of confidence and a bit of a swagger; *this'll impress him,* I thought to myself. However, now that I've been at it for about ten minutes, it has become apparent that I am making no progress at all with my "Quick, swim across the bay"; in fact, I have a sense of moving backwards. It must be something to do with currents or tides. I wish now that I had entered the water from the other end of the beach, as I would be hacking along like an Olympian, and Martin would be gobsmacked by my athletic abilities. Anyway, it doesn't matter what Martin thinks...does it? I give this some thought. In truth the whole thing is probably in my head. I don't know him well, but I do know that he is more interested in studying the local semi-naked beauties wandering about on the beach than in his middle-aged gay brother flapping about in the waves.

Admitting defeat and pretending I didn't intend to swim very far anyway, I tread water and turn my attention towards my mum. Her head is gently moving as her gaze follows a young couple energetically making their way along the prom with walking poles and a small dog. She is obviously commenting on them, as my dad has suddenly looked up and is also following their progress. I wonder what theory she has about them. A holiday romance? A sordid affair? I can't see their footwear, but I would like to think their shoes will have influenced her thinking in some way.

As I watch her watching them, I reflect on our ill-fated conversations of earlier this week, and I feel a sense of guilt and regret. Like me just a few minutes ago, she must have felt scrutinised, but it wasn't in her imagination – it was real, and it was cutting.

As I tread water, I step into her shoes for a moment (pale pink Skechers to match her lippy) and try to imagine things from her perspective...

...I imagine that I am struggling to make sense of the world around me; things don't seem to quite connect as I think maybe they should do. People and places are familiar, but it can be difficult to name them or remember how they relate to each other or to me. I add to this the idea that people around me, the very people I love and trust, are studying me, looking out for me to make a mistake, to expose a weakness, and in doing so prove that I am less of a person than I was six months ago...

Wow...that is too harsh to contemplate without sinking below the surface – I head for shore.

* * *

Later in the week, thankfully, any leftover emotions seem to have dissipated. Mum and I are back to our old selves; a mother and son who love each other very much and enjoy a solid relationship built on dignity, respect, and trust. I am relieved and appreciate what we have.

There is nothing wrong with asking how people are doing; in fact it's important – but it's the way in which you ask and the nature of your intentions that can be damaging. Lesson learnt.

Another thing I have learnt today is that naked foam Parties in Ayia Napa are seasonal, and I am relieved to discover our visit is out of season.

* * *

It's our last night in Cyprus, and we are sitting in a bar having a few drinks. The conversation is focused on Martin, as a youngster, who was always a bit of a handful. He seemed to reach puberty not long after he was house-trained and as a result was on the lookout for romance, and *maybe more*, from a startlingly early age. This issue was further complicated by the fact that we lived in a small village where everybody knew each other, so Mum and Dad had to contend with him trying to establish romantic connections with the daughters of most, if not all their friends. To add to this, being an open-minded and inclusive kind of chap, he didn't discriminate against anybody, so if he failed to impress the daughters, he tried his luck with their mothers.

This situation was not easy for our parents to manage, as Martin was a young man on a mission, and he kept his eye firmly on the prize. Apparently, they had to contend with the same kind of problem with Carny the farting Labrador. He had similar inclinations, but his affections were aimed at other dogs, sheep, and an unfortunate, but very attractive, tortoise. The difference was that they could have Carny "Schmackled" (an Essex word for castrated), which at least slowed him down for a while. This wasn't an option with Martin of course... although I do wonder if it was considered.

Not wanting Martin to get all the glory in this conversation, my dad then shifts the focus to me and mentions the day he (allegedly) saw a man in a dress climbing out of my bedroom window. I have no memory of this, and I'm pretty sure I would remember. But, having all had a few drinks, my protests are ignored and the hilarity of it all continues.

Then Mum looks at me and says, "Well..." (Her pause suggests a bombshell is coming.) "What about the time you had your hair permed and your dad had to go up to the school and apologise!"

Bloody hell! How could she introduce this excruciating incident that I have worked so hard to erase from my memory? I thought we were allies!

I was thirteen years old – already being bullied at school – and had the bright idea that a perm would make everything OK – needless to say, it did not...

By this point in the conversation, Martin and Mum are almost crying with laughter. Martin then struggles to mention my pre-school ironing board obsession, but he can't get the words out, for which I am thankful. I'm so pleased Simon isn't with us – I'm not sure he has heard many of these stories. Wondering what they will come out with next, I try and shift the focus back to my brother, who has far more dodgy events in his back catalogue than I do, but before I get a chance, my dad looks at me and says, "Well..." (Oh God, here we go again.) "What about the Dobbs Weir fiasco!" Martin has no memory of this incident, and as it is a story of bravery and adventure, for which I have some belated pride, I agree to tell it in a last-ditch attempt to earn back a little self-respect.

* * *

It was summer term, and I was seven or eight years old. Sports day was coming up, which, for me, was the worst day of the entire year. My teacher, Mrs. H, had decided who was being entered for which event – high jump, long jump, running races, sack races, etc. I was not an athletic child. I couldn't catch, throw, kick, jump, or run, so overall I was a bad choice for anything. However, as with past years, I seemed to be entered into every event. This particular year, the thought of sports day had been keeping me awake at night. It filled my small chest with the familiar tight fist of dread that overpowered all my time and thoughts. Looking back, I think it was the fear of failure and humiliation as well as a total lack of confidence in my physical ability. On top of that, I just didn't like being forced to do anything, particularly if I thought it was rubbish. Which it was.

It was Monday morning, and it was *practice day*. This was a new idea, which was described by Mrs. H as a "Full dress rehearsal for sports day" ... "Which means we will have twice the fun!"

I wasn't buying this – it made no sense. It's like doing something you have been really dreading for ages and then, you finally get it out of the way, only to discover that, in fact, you must do it all again, but this time with an audience. I felt like a loser, which due to my natural ability and lack of confidence, I most certainly was. The idea of being a double loser filled me with angst, particularly when I knew from experience that Mrs. H, *always supportive*, had a habit of pointing out my and my fellow losers' weaknesses for everyone to enjoy and "learn from!" This reflective exercise resulted in any morsel of self-assurance I may have conjured up being quickly stamped out and extinguished with great gusto.

Through my child's-eye view of life, this fast-approaching event cast an all-encompassing shadow, which I could not avoid or see beyond. This may sound a little dramatic, and in the grand scheme of things not so terrible, but cast your mind back to being a youngster. What was important? What were your worries? How big was your world? To me, at that time, this was a frightening thing to contemplate; I guess Mrs. H and her obsession with sports day was another manifestation of the dark threat that lurked in *Pogles' Wood*.

* * *

As I set off for school that Monday morning, the sun was shining, so even my hopes of being rained off had come to nothing. I could feel the expanding fist of fear opening and pushing its fingers through my young ribs. Looking back, I wonder why I didn't make out I was ill and try and get the day off – if anything warranted that kind of devious, but sensible, behaviour, it was sports day. But for some reason I didn't want to be the kid who feared sports, although I knew deep down that I most definitely was. In fact, just the sight of a football or the sound of somebody shouting "Catch!" or "Get the ball for us, mate!" is still likely to result in me stumbling about and missing the ball while mumbling apologies. So as a result of this, I give people playing ball games a very wide berth and walk across sports fields in giant arcs of avoidance...but still they call..."Throw the ball back to us, mate!"

I walked past the old air raid shelter that we sometimes used as a den. Its red brick entrance with concrete lintel looked so safe, dark, and inviting. The ideal place to disappear. I wished I was inside sitting on the little WWII camp bed listening to my transistor radio through its tiny cream earplug. But I wasn't. I was going to school to spend the day feeling humiliated and useless.

My mind was in turmoil: *Why do I have to do this? Why do I even have to go to school? Why can't I stay at home with Carny the farting Labrador and listen to Mum's stories of goats and goblins? Maybe I could even overcome my past problems and once again pick up my knitting needles and have a lovely life adrift on the orange rug.*

The next thing I knew I was crouched down behind a wooden pallet in the dark and dusty air raid shelter. I don't remember planning it, or even my decision to do it. This was my first real experience of fight or flight, and I had clearly opted for flight. I was living in the moment and doing what was right at that precise time in my young life. I hid there for ages. I can still smell the thick dust mixed with a sniff of mouse, old hessian sacks, and lorry drivers' pee.

When things started to settle and my Captain Scarlet watch with luminous hands told me that this was now official – school had started – I began to ponder what to do next.

In my head, Mrs. H was taking the register and calling my name over and over again, getting louder and louder:

"Where is Marcus?"

"Where is MARCUS?"

"WHERE IS MARCUS?"

A long hour later, I snuck out across the fields and made

my way to the river. I was nervous but at the same time exhilarated. It was good to realise that, despite the things that were taking place at school that morning, the rest of the world was continuing as normal. The river slowly flowed, dragon flies buzzed around, the water rats scampered along the bank in quick flashes, and the swans moved silently and gently through the current.

I was free. My nerves were gradually calming, and I was beginning to enjoy this feeling of taking control and having the prospect of a long, hot summer's day ahead of me. And at that age the days were very, very long. So, any thoughts of what might happen later that night, when I would be discovered, didn't really bother me because it was a lifetime away.

What followed was a week-and-a-half odyssey of getting up in the morning, dressing for school, walking three miles to a place called Dobbs Weir, and hiding under a willow tree whose leaves reached down and dipped into the water. I ate a Twix bar for my lunch, then I would walk home at the usual time, pretending I'd been at school. My memory of those days is of time going slowly, feeling hungry, but also feeling released from all that stuff that worried me. I was clearly living in the moment, rather than thinking about the future.

Looking back, it's weird that the teachers didn't contact my parents, but it was a little village school in the early seventies, and I guess they didn't bother back then. Renee Batterbury would only keep her boys away from school if there was a good reason, so life went on and nothing was said.

Then one evening I bumped into my friends Steven and Stephen, who were eager to know why I was off school. So, without thinking I told them that I had been rushed to hospital to have my appendix out. This is something that had happened to a cousin, and I thought it sounded very dramatic and convincing. I mean, who would make up something like that? For them this was both exciting and blood-curdling in equal measures, and of course they were desperate to see my scar and stitches.

Damn! I put them off somehow but arranged to meet them the following day and promised to show them the gory evidence.

Next day, when I got home from the willow tree, I took a thick roll of sticking plaster from the bathroom cabinet and went to my bedroom. I cut a large rectangle off the roll and stuck a big ball of cotton wool in the middle of it. Then I squeezed half a tube of red paint and half a tube of yellow paint over the cotton wool; I then topped the whole thing off with a squirt of pink Germolene. Once this oily trifle was complete, I carefully turned the whole thing over and stuck it to my stomach where I imagined my appendix should be. As I gently pushed on the plaster to ensure it had stuck, I think I realised that I was on the jagged edge, and this may well be the beginning of the end.

A little later, as arranged, I met up with Steven and Stephen. They were eager and excited to see my scar and stitches. I warned them that the operation hadn't gone that well, and it was a bit of a mess, so I wasn't sure if the stitches were visible. This only served to add to their enthusiasm. So as requested I slowly peeled back the plaster. Thick red blood and yellow puss oozed out and dribbled down my fingers and stomach, and it just kept coming. The Germolene made the whole gory mess look putrid, serious, and smell medical. Looking down and realising that this didn't really look as convincing as I imagined it would, I very quickly covered it up again, "Just in case something falls out."

This amazing display of drama and creativity was not only much more impressive than winning any sack race (sports day was now all in the past), but, unfortunately, was also the key to my downfall. Poor Steven and Stephen were so traumatised by their experience, and my heroic stiff upper lip, that they couldn't stop talking about it. Well, either that or they instantly saw through my ploy, which, looking back, is the most likely. Anyway, one thing led to another, and after a week and a half of walking on the wild side, I was found out.

* * *

I can't help smiling with pride as I tell Martin, Mum, and Dad about this event, but rest assured, at the time it was a very difficult experience. My parents were completely shocked by what had happened. Skipping school was something teenagers did, not eight-year-old boys who were scared of their own shadow. I felt like I was now in an overwhelming amount of trouble and was dreading what might come next.

But it turned out that my parents weren't angry; they were concerned, upset, and bewildered, but there were no tears or telling off. They did, however, need to understand what was going on, so they did two things I will always be grateful for: The first thing they did was ask me, calmly, respectfully and with love, why I had felt the need to do something so out of character and desperate. The second thing they did was listen to and take on board what I had to say. I can't really remember a great deal about the conversation. I know I did tell them the headlines, that I was dreading school, etc. But I also know I didn't mention sports day, even to them. It's a little sad to think that even at that age I found not being sporty so shameful that I just couldn't bring myself to say it out loud.

My dad, who I believe was, and still is, secretly impressed with my daring adventure, went to the school the next morning and did all he could to make sure my behaviour was understood, and the real question was what had triggered me to do this, particularly five or six years earlier than he had when he was a boy. Overall, whatever he said did the trick and, on my return, I was left in relative peace by the teachers – including Mrs. H. However, the other kids did make comments and call me names, which, looking back, surprises me as I think my little escapade was heroic compared to any rubbish egg and spoon race.

My mum was, as always, full of love and reassurance that everything would be OK. From then on, she took extra care to ensure we regularly spoke about how things were at school. I think she realised that there was more going on for me – even before I did. In my memory this was the start of a different kind of relationship between us – at this point we became allies to each other, which is something we have continued to be right through to the moment she dropped the perm bomb earlier this evening – for which I am still struggling to truly forgive her.

This isn't the only example of our parents responding to *bad* behaviour in an unexpected way. Reflecting on it now, I realise how forgiving and supportive they have been to the two of us. On this occasion it would have been so much easier for them to tell me off, apologise to the school and agree to some kind of mindless punishment. This had the potential to be a really awful time, and in my young world, I couldn't see a way forwards, but they were reassuring, they listened to, and heard, what I had to say and then supported me. As I share this story, on our last evening in Cyprus, I tell them how much I appreciate the way they handled this challenging (and impressive) incident.

Mum chips in and says she remembers this event very well; she also adds a few humorous details that may, or may not, be factual. She then says something poignant: "If somebody in your family is struggling or needs help – it's really important to stop and listen to what they are saying – that's the only way you can make things better."

We have had a great evening – with lots more stories I will not repeat here, but rest assured that I did tip the balance and move the focus back to Martin and his many adventures. It is so funny to hear Mum and Dad talking about their perspective on the trials and tribulations of trying to raise us to the best of their abilities.

I think they did OK...despite everything.

Mum says she often used to ask herself: "Why can't I just have a normal family like other people?"

* * *

Overall, the holiday has been an enormous success. We all had the opportunity and time to reconnect with each other; Martin and I were able to start to build a relationship as grown-ups (notice I didn't say adults), and I was reminded by my mum of the importance of treating the people I love with dignity and respect. We reminisced about the past and generally did a lot of laughing – mostly at each other's, or other people's expense.

Flying home, I sit next to Mum. After some time spent looking out of the window and commenting on the clouds, she turns to me and asks where we have been and where are we going, because she has forgotten. When I remind her, it all comes flooding back, and then we settle down to make up stories about our fellow passengers. One of which she is convinced is a doctor, because he has "beautiful healing hands and expensive shoes."

Risky Business

My dad is staying with us for a few days, as he and his best mate John are going to a car show just along the coast from where we live. They do this a couple of times a year. Mum is OK staying at home, she has everything she needs, and he phones her morning and evening to check all is well. At this point, I'm happy to say, her condition does not encroach on her confidence or ability to be home alone for a day or two. In fact, she seems proud that she can "take care of the household, while Guy has some time with John." This is impressive.

It's been nearly a year since our holiday to Cyprus, and I'm happy to report that very few of my list of *what ifs* have come to fruition. It appears that the progression of Mum's illness is very slow compared to some other people; I suppose that is the nature of the beast – you never quite know how it will develop and affect each individual. But for us life has continued, with its ups, downs, and steady states, taking things one day at a time, and living in the moment.

On Dad's first night with us, as is our tradition, I cook a pasta bake with garlic bread, and the three of us get slowly trollied on gin and wine. These little soirees are always fun and have a slightly different feel to them because the family party animal, my mum, isn't there – not in person anyway.

Simon is a great one for buying vinyl records, either from record shops in Brighton or from charity shops. This means that he has a very large and broad collection of music – some horrendous and some fabulous. Tonight, he is testing mine and Dad's musical knowledge by putting on mystery tracks while, drunkenly and ineffectively, hiding the record sleeves. It's surprising how good we are as a team of two. From the soundtrack to *Jungle Book* (a record that should be a part of every kid's upbringing), and crooners such as Matt Munroe and Tony Bennet, to seventies superstars The Stylistics, and eighties hits like "Genius of Love" by Tom Tom Club, between us, me and my dad have managed not only to identify most tracks, but due to my delusional red wine-induced confidence, I am even able to sing along to some of them – which must be a treat for my two companions.

Between records, I pop up to the bathroom and catch a glimpse of my reflection in the mirror – that familiar *Joker*-like red wine grin is stretched almost from ear to ear, and there is also a generous red spillage down the front of my T-shirt – two reliable signs that I am in a good place and a little too excited with life.

When I get back downstairs, Olivia Newton John is singing about being hopelessly devoted to John Travolta. I momentarily think, *Hoorah! I know the words!* But when I enter the room, my dad is telling Simon about his life-long love and admiration for Olivia and how this came to a head when he took Mum, Joy and John to see her in concert at the Rainbow Theatre, London. Just like Mum and her dreams of Johnny Mathis, Dad was half convinced he and Olivia may have a romantic future together (I assume when they said their marriage vows there was a caveat about running off with Johnny or Olivia should the opportunity arise).

My dad loved the concert; it was the musical highlight of his life...which is more than what can be said for Joy and John, who, being ardent classic jazz enthusiasts, were not impressed at all. Their opinions and discomfort were exacerbated when Dad, getting caught up in the spirit of "Let's Get Physical," ran down to the front and danced his heart out with the youngsters.

It took several years for Joy and John to completely recover and forgive my dad for this episode – but the fact that he and John are still best mates forty years later, and now, in their late seventies, are going to car shows and gushing over Formula 1 drivers does say something about the strength of their friendship.

* * *

In addition to taking a couple of days away and spending some time with us, these visits also provide the opportunity for my dad to speak openly and honestly about how *he* is doing, which is important, because his wife isn't the only one living with her dementia. We encourage him to be open and talk about the situation candidly, asking what daily life is like, not only for Mum but also for him. These kinds of questions open the door to a place where it's OK to talk about the challenges and struggles as well as the successes he is experiencing. In our current situation it's easy to focus all our attention on Mum, but his wellbeing is of equal, if not more importance, as he is the one who creates an environment that enables his wife to live as well as she can.

He does share that at times, it is indeed difficult and he finds it hard to handle. Talking about this is not easy, and as he verbalises his experiences there is an air of guilt as if it's a bad thing to speak about, but in fact it is the opposite – it is vital for him to be able to share these feelings and thoughts. It doesn't mean he loves her any less, it just means that sometimes, it is tough being him.

Although in his late seventies, Dad still works three days a week. His place of work is a one-hour drive each way, and his job is interesting and busy, with people he needs to talk to, and a few good friends. I think he is very brave going off to work and leaving his wife alone, but the truth is that although there are associated risks and there have been one or two small mishaps, these are far outweighed by the psychological benefits for them both. For my mum – being trusted by her husband and reaffirming for herself that she can get through the day independently. And for Dad, getting some respite, talking to other people, and reassuring himself that he isn't de-skilling his wife by being there all the time and doing everything for her. He says that although being with her constantly might be the safest option, it would knock her confidence and her self-belief...and would most likely irritate her. I think he might be right.

This positive risk-taking isn't the easy option. It is the opposite; it is the hard option – but in their unique situation, at this point, it feels like the right thing to do. Simon is intrigued to know how this works. What if she forgets he is at work and starts searching for him? Or if something comes up that is unexpected and causes her to get anxious? Dad explains that she has his mobile number written on the wall by the phone, and she does call him regularly, and yes sometimes she wants to know where he is and why he isn't at home. But once he reminds her and reassures her that he will be back at a certain time, she regains her confidence and plays down her concerns. He adds that she also has close neighbours she can call on, and she spends a significant amount of time on the phone to her sister.

He then goes on to talk about her *Information Station*, in the kitchen.

* * *

Ever since I can remember, there has been a calendar hanging on the kitchen wall of my parents' home. There was one in our tiny bungalow in Roydon, which, when I was a youngster, I used to count down the days to school holidays (longing to escape to a better world). Meanwhile, Mum used it to record significant appointments, events, birthdays, and details of her diet – for example: *No Bread Today!*

All these years later, there is still a calendar hanging on the kitchen wall, but now it's in their house in Clacton. The calendar has a spring at the top, a page for each month and a line for each day, and it is used for the same things (except diet details and, thankfully, school term dates). This has always been Mum's *go-to* place, to remind her what is happening and when. As time has moved on and her dementia has become more of an issue, this simple port of call has become increasingly important. This is such a good thing – her habit of heading to the kitchen when she gets up in the morning and on numerous occasions throughout the day enables her to feel a little more independent and ask fewer questions.

All the information on the calendar has been added by Mum, sometimes with her husband's prompting, and other times not. For example, at the beginning of each week she will ask him which days he is working, what time he will leave in the morning and what time he will be home. Likewise, at the start of each New Year, she will add all the family birthdays using the previous year's calendar as a guide. In this case, my dad will read out the details and she will fill in the date and name. The fact that she recognises her own handwriting when she visits the calendar adds an extra layer of control and ownership of what is happening.

Filling in each day also provides an opportunity for her to use her reading and writing skills, of which she is very proud. This may all sound a bit mundane – this focusing on small details – but it is important and beneficial – this is about making the most of her strengths and abilities. If somebody else, for example my dad, filled in the calendar and presented it to her each month, it would be a different experience. It would be a timetable of events that are being done *to* her – which could reduce her sense of pride in being organised – and remember, she has always done this; it's how she has planned and ordered her life. Of course, there may well come a time when somebody else does need to do the writing, but if this happens it won't be the end of the world; we just need to ensure it is being done *with* her, using her language, and giving her the information that is important to her.

Dad goes on to explain that over the past few months he has noticed that she is spending more and more time studying what has been written, and as she does this, she is asking more questions – for example, "What day is it?" and "What date is it?" She is looking for one of those *You Are Here!* arrows that you find on maps in car parks. Once she knows where she is on the calendar, she can understand what is happening.

Up until recently, she has used the daily newspaper to get the day and date information, but this doesn't seem to be happening now unless my dad prompts her. To remedy this, he has had a great idea – he has bought a large square clock which hangs at eye level next to the calendar. The clock has a clear face with hands and numbers, the day, the date and even the year. Initially, when it was first installed Mum would continue to ask those key questions, but rather than give her the answer (the simple option), he nudged her to look at the clock as that will tell her all she needs to know. Over time this is becoming a part of her routine. This simple strategy has helped her keep her sense of self-reliance, and that is priceless. Moving forwards things may change, but for the moment this is working...most of the time.

On the days when he does go to work, Dad will leave after breakfast in the morning and get home mid-afternoon. This is particularly important in the winter when the days are short, as he wants to avoid Mum being home alone after dark. He explains to us that his employers are fully aware of his circumstances, and he has an agreement that he may swap or cancel working days at short notice. He has made it very clear to them that although he enjoys his job, his wife's welfare is his priority. They obviously have a great deal of respect for him because they support this 100%.

Both Simon and I are amazed at his pragmatic approach to these issues. Most of the strategies he uses are very practical, simple, and obvious. But I'm not sure they would have occurred to me. Another important point that seems to come naturally to him is that he doesn't assume Mum has lost skills and abilities just because of her dementia. In his eyes she is able until proven otherwise, and even then, what is impossible today may be possible tomorrow.

* * *

It's the day of his departure, and Dad calls Mum while we are eating breakfast. All three of us have a chat with her. I can hear the sense of achievement in her voice. She slept well and the sun is shining in Clacton-on-Sea, but I can also detect a slight edge of relief. She is OK, and Guy will be heading home later today. When the phone is handed to Simon, with an air of mischief in his voice he asks if she is looking forward to seeing Guy this afternoon. I hear her say through a smirk that she is looking forward to seeing him, but she's pleased he won't be back until later because, "At the moment my fancy man is in the kitchen making me a cup of tea and some toast!" They go on to discuss fancy men and handsome doctors – one of their staple subjects of conversation.

After the call, we talk about the fact that Dad's approach to positive risk-taking has a fine balance to it. He tells us he is certainly not complacent or even relaxed about it. He is always ready to change or cancel his plans if needed. He says that he realises that in time as her condition progresses, he may well need to leave work and stay home. He doesn't have a problem with that, and he will do whatever it takes to support her, but he isn't going to solve that potential problem until it is a reality and there is a genuine need. He isn't inventing futures here. He is, as usual, living with Mum in the moment, taking each day as it comes while occasionally scanning the horizon.

One Small Step, and One Giant Leap

September 9th, 2012. I am woken at three a.m. by my phone that lets me know I have a message. I have recently signed up for the International Space Station (ISS) mailing list, and I am being given the heads up that I will be able to see it pass across the sky this evening. The fact that the message arrives in the middle of the night makes me wonder about the crew living life in orbit above the Earth. I am curious to know how they manage their time. They are constantly passing over time zones, but which one are they tethered to? Or do they have their own? In addition to this, I am wondering if the space station travels with or against the rotation of the Earth. Humans are creatures of habit, and our bodies seem to be programmed to function in cycles of hours and days, so it must be quite a challenge keeping the body clock in check. As I doze, I make a mental note to find out more about this in the morning.

Later on, with a cup of tea in my hand and Google at my fingertips, I discover the crew of the ISS witness sixteen sunrises and sixteen sunsets in twenty-four hours, but to keep a regular schedule they use Greenwich Mean Time (GMT). They do not work day and night shifts, as I assumed they would, but instead they all have a similar routine getting up at 6:30 and going to bed around 21:30. They are travelling with the rotation of the Earth, which is west to east. It would be possible to travel in orbit in the opposite direction, but it's more complicated. That's all my questions answered – for now. I just love this stuff and am excited to think that later today we may see a spaceship containing real live astronauts flying across the sky high above our garden in Lancing, England. It will appear at 20:02 tonight.

Hitting Google again, I learn that it takes the ISS about seven minutes to cross from the horizon in the west to its opposite horizon in the east. During that time, it will travel about 2,000 miles at a speed of 17,150 mph. Unbelievably, ninety to ninety-three minutes later it will reappear in the west again, having travelled right around the world! Wow, what a wonderful thing to happen; I am keeping my fingers crossed for a clear night sky.

* * *

Today is not just a day to look out for spaceships; it is also Mum's eightieth birthday. To celebrate, she and Dad are staying with us for a few days. The weather is good, and there is still some warmth in the sun, so we are taking a walk along the seafront. We stop and buy a coffee and ice cream from a takeaway and sit in a row on a bench facing the sea. As usual on her birthday, Mum is questioning her age, and today she is struggling to believe she really is eighty.

"But why would we lie?" I ask in exasperation.

"Well, I can remember being sixteen, and it doesn't seem that long ago."

I tell her that time flies when you're having fun.

She turns to her husband. "We have had some fun, haven't we, Guy? Remember all those pub lock-ins?"

"Too well," he replies.

They are now reminiscing about a particular evening, or rather very early morning, when the doors were locked in the pub; their friend Eileen, the landlady, had set up a little buffet, and they all enjoyed a few too many drinks. At some point during the night, the local police constabulary pulled up in their car outside the pub and peered in through the gaps in the curtains. They couldn't see much, but they could certainly hear lots of laughter, and Ralph, another dear friend, singing Welsh hymns very loudly in his impressively deep baritone. Whether it was the sight of half a dozen near-hysterical women knocking back the Cinzanos while their husbands slurped their pints, or maybe it was the view of a group of close friends having a fun but harmless party, or it could even have been the sound of Ralph's passionate singing giving the impression of some kind of religious event taking place, whatever it was, something made the local bobbies think better of it and drive away.

At the end of the night, Mum and Dad, along with Ralph and his wife Joyce, strode confidently out of the door and headed towards home. It was a good few minutes before any of them realised they were heading in completely the wrong direction. After much laughter and cackling, they redirected themselves and, once again, made their way safely back to the bungalow. This is the first time Simon has heard this story, and we are all laughing as Mum adds more and more embellishments for his benefit, and to demonstrate just how drunk they really were. There is an element of emotion at the mention of dear old Ralph and his wonderful singing voice. Eventually we calm down and turn our attention to our now-melting ice creams.

"So what day is it?"

A chorus: "It's your birthday!"

"Is it! Well, how old am I?"

And the conversation continues until Simon saves the day. "I tell you what, Renee, you may be eighty, but you still look twenty-one."

She stands up and, with a smile, does a little wiggle. "Thank you, darlin'."

* * *

Later, we are sitting at the table, dinner eaten, candles blown out, and wishes made. My brother Martin has called to wish Mum a happy birthday and she is content, feeling loved and sipping a glass of Lambrini. I say sipping, but she empties the glass in a few swift gulps. She's never been one for sipping; life's too short. What with her flirty bottom wiggle earlier and her liberal approach to her drink, Renee, of pub lock-in fame, is still very much with us in the here and now on her eightieth birthday!

I check my watch – 19:55. "Actually, you've got one more surprise. I've arranged for the International Space Station to fly over to say happy birthday."

"You are daft," she replies, not at all taken in by what I've said.

We all head outside, and we know exactly where to look for it to appear. My mum has amazing eyesight, so she and Simon take charge of scanning the horizon. Although she's not sure what it is we are looking for, she can tell we are excited about the prospect of it appearing, so she embraces the search.

I check my watch again. "OK, it's time."

We all look west, and as if by magic, the Space Station appears, over the treetops. Too big to be a satellite, moving at a certain speed and pace that strangely sets it aside from any aircraft, majestic in its confidence and direction, but there is also an air of extreme and tiny isolation about it. It is a wonderful thing to see.

"So are there people in that thing?" asks Mum.

But before we have time to answer, my dad chips in, "Well, which one is it?" We all look at him.

"There are two; how do you know which one it is?" he asks seriously.

His question is destined to go down in our family history as he is only one gin and tonic down and is already seeing double!

It's amazing, to look up at this tiny object out in space that has men and women doing their science and maybe, just maybe, looking down on us. I flash my torch with made-up morse code, just in case.

* * *

Back indoors I am sharing my memories of the day that Neil Armstrong walked on the moon. I was only five, but I seem to have a clear memory of our family all trouping outside of our little bungalow to look up and see Apollo 11 chasing the moon in the clear night sky. My memory tells me it looked like a bright star edging ever closer to its destination.

Mum and Dad have no memory of this event and, although it is my truth, it feels very unlikely to be factual. If it did happen, I would assume the rocket was far closer to the Earth than I thought. I wonder where this memory came from. It's so real and clear in my mind. Maybe the fuzzy television pictures had been bought to life by my imagination, or maybe, just maybe, it did happen, and I am the only one to remember it. I hope that is the case; I love having my own private memory of seeing a space rocket.

One thing is for sure: I can't watch that film clip of Neil Armstrong taking "One small step for man and one giant leap for mankind," without thinking to myself...*I saw that rocket...I witnessed history.*

As I tell this story, I am trying to remember the name of the music that my memory tells me was used in the TV coverage of the space missions – Simon looks it up, and by the wonder of technology in seconds, Richard Strauss. *Also sprach Zarathustra,* Op. 30, no. 1, "Prelude," is filling the room.

Just hearing this piece of music sends a shiver down my spine and takes me back to that time looking up through my child's eyes and watching a rocket chase the moon.

Strangely enough this is the first time I have ever questioned if this story is based on a true event. Over the years I have told various people about it, and now I am wondering if they believed me. I'm not going to look for evidence or validation; I like this memory, it's my truth and I am sticking with it. I am my mother's son.

* * *

Talking of steps, we've had some significant steps take place in our family over the past eighteen months.

Although she has always been active, in the last year of her seventies Mum's mobility started to noticeably decrease. She was struggling to get out of the chair, had developed a slight limp and avoided walking as much as possible. This was completely out of character because her normal default setting has always been to keep moving. In fact, she normally finds it hard to sit still for any length of time. But it was becoming increasingly clear that she was experiencing pain in her hip or leg.

Around this time, she and Dad came down from Essex to stay with us in our new home. This was the first time they had visited, and I was excited to show them around and show them the garden. Having always lived in a flat, this was our first garden, and although it was just a rectangle of grass, we had great plans, but at that point, we were just happy to step out of the back door onto the grass.

As their car pulled up outside, Mum, uncharacteristically, stayed put. I opened the passenger door and was shocked to see her struggling to get out. She then needed me and Simon on either side of her to help her walk to the front door and into the lounge. I was amazed how quickly her mobility had deteriorated.

Despite her reluctance to ever acknowledge being unwell, she was talking about this particular issue openly, although I must point out that when she did mention it, she blamed it on having been sitting down for too long or laying on the wrong side in bed. Then, true to form, she added her much repeated line, "I'm not ill, and I won't let anybody tell me that I am." This, as usual, was said in a way that very clearly puts a full stop on the subject. Her stoic approach, probably inherited from her mum, is admirable, but it does make things tricky when we are trying to get her to agree to see a doctor. It's strange that despite her life-long love and respect for the medical profession, she is not very keen on having anything to do with them, particularly when the focus is on her own health. My dad had already had what he described as "a few false starts." Meaning that Mum had agreed in principle to visit the GP but then refused at the last minute; but they did eventually reach a fragile compromise. He achieved this by pointing out that, "As you know from working in the NHS, pain in the hip is not an illness, but it is inconvenient, so maybe the doctor can give you something to take away the pain." This subtle reminder about her connection with the NHS, something that she is very proud of, enabled her to see this through a slightly different lens, one where she has control, knowledge, and value. This sounds like a small detail, but it was very effective in shifting her view, and at last she agreed to visit the GP...albeit reluctantly.

Having spoken to the GP, they then soon found themselves talking to a surgeon. Following an examination and X-rays, he confirmed what we had suspected – Mum needed hip replacements; otherwise she would soon be using a wheelchair. This was not the news she expected or wanted to hear, and her natural respect for him wavered. She was not convinced or even interested in having any kind of surgery. In fact, she flatly refused and went into denial, insisting there was no problem. Meanwhile, his wheelchair comment hit the reality button for my dad, and his future was flashing before his eyes. Mum would not make a good wheelchair user and would really struggle being reliant on others. Thoughts about home also bombarded him. Would this mean she couldn't get around the house? Would he need to get a stair lift installed, and what if...the list of *what ifs* started spiralling out of control.

Then with a jolt he was bought back into the moment when, without realising it, the wonderful surgeon pulled the ace card out of the hat. Combining Mum's two top obsessions (once again the NHS, but this time with the addition of the royal family) he said, "I think you deserve new hips, all paid for by the NHS, and why shouldn't you have them? The Queen Mother has two new hips, and you are just as important as her."

Taken aback, Mum looked at her husband. "Has she really, Guy? Has the Queen Mother really got new hips?"

Once the royal hip situation had been confirmed by my dad and, just to be sure, a nearby nurse, there was a sudden miraculous U-turn. That was it; the deal was done. Just a simple blue-blooded statement from a medical professional resulted in a potentially life-changing decision being made.

"Well, of course I'll get new hips; why wouldn't I? If the Queen Mother's got some, I'd better get some too!" And that was that.

Meanwhile for me, the news of her needing surgery was devastating. I felt like we were in a no-win situation. Without the surgery she would lose her independence and maybe her dignity. She may have even lost her spark for life (although this is doubtful). But she was already struggling with her memory, and we knew from experience that any traumatic event could possibly advance her condition, and having watched a hip replacement operation on YouTube, I felt that this fitted very well into the *traumatic event* category. In fact, just watching it on a laptop was harrowing enough.

So, I felt that surgery and the likely confusion and disorientation this may well incur would all be too much for my mum and, to be frank, I convinced myself that this could be the beginning of the end. However, I knew that I had invented a future that didn't actually exist, so I kept my worries to myself. I didn't even talk to Simon about them, as usual – saying it aloud would just make it a bit too *real* for me to deal with.

* * *

As the date of surgery approached, I drove up to Essex to see how things were going. That morning before I arrived, Mum and Dad had got up very early, driven to Colchester and attended a group workshop exploring and practicing essential post-op exercises and stretches. This, as it turned out, was a funny experience, as Mum seemed to have some hidden talents when it came to swinging her legs and wiggling her midriff. She clearly enjoyed being able to do this properly, and the invaluable positive feedback from the physiotherapist gave her a sense of achievement (yet another example of the power of strengths-based feedback). My dad, however, was not so used to making these flamboyant moves. He was wobbling about all over the place and wondering what he'd got himself into.

Apparently, there was much hilarity amongst the group as Mum, the person having her hips replaced, commenced teaching her husband, the only person in the group not having surgery, how to do the moves. Of course, having an audience, she made a bit of a show of it and added a certain style, and panache, to her demonstrations. My poor dad! He does not enjoy attention, but he just grinned, swallowed his pride and tolerated it – no doubt keeping his mind very much on the greater good.

When they played this back to me, despite the laughter, I was very aware of the real hero of this story – my amazing dad, and Mum's amazing husband, who will do anything for love. The outcome of this double-edged event was that it seemed to have given them both an injection of positivity and vitality – they had something tangible they could do to improve the situation. They had some influence and an element of control.

I love how my dad volunteered to join in with this. His thinking was that if they did the exercises together, there was a better chance of Mum sticking to the regime, making a full recovery, and, crucially, getting the full use of her legs back. In addition to this, his recent wobbly experience had convinced him that he would probably benefit from the exercises to keep his original *old school* hips in good shape!

Despite all this positivity, and the hilarity of their early morning antics, if I'm honest, the prospect of my mum's approaching surgery still made me feel like a dark cloud was descending over us, and to complete a much-used cliché, I really couldn't see any kind of silver lining. I was struggling to figure out why I felt so pessimistic. My character naturally errs on the side of positive thinking and making things as good as they can be. On reflection I think maybe I was feeling powerless. By nature, I am a bit of a rescuer, and I try to make everything perfect, which I'm sure can be irritating, but I do mean well. However, this wasn't possible. There wasn't anyone I could call to sort things out, or anything I could buy to make things easier. All I could do was try to keep up an encouraging and supportive front, so at least my dark thoughts weren't affecting my parents, who, true to nature, were just getting on with it.

Mum's short-term memory loss meant that she regularly needed reminding what was going to be happening. This doesn't mean that there was a need for a constant barrage of reminders, which were not necessary, but when there was a good reason to talk about the upcoming surgery, there was a very real risk she would experience increased anxiety and become agitated. However, to avoid this happening, my brilliant dad introduced the subject by reminding her about the conversation with the surgeon, adding the fact that it had been all her decision, and then praised her bravery, pointing out that he was not sure he would have the courage if the shoe was on the other foot. This simple approach put Mum in the driving seat, whereby she could ask for any details she needed, and invariably it was clear that she was proud of herself for having the confidence to take this giant step towards a different future.

Again, this was all very much being done *with* her and not *to* her, and once she adopted this frame of mind there was no stopping her; "Well as you know, I have known surgeons and doctors all my life, and they certainly wouldn't do this if they didn't think it was needed." Then, in a half whisper, she would add a *Renee elaboration*, "Actually, the surgeon took me to one side and asked me to go ahead with the surgery so he can practice as he hasn't done it before, and he knows I would be a top patient and do all the exercises."

She was speaking from a place of belief and empowerment. It is highly unlikely that he said that to her, but maybe he did! And who cares? She was feeling good.

The following day, as I drove home, I came to realise that the dark cloud with no silver lining was my own invention – it was the manifestation of my insecurities, and my fears. As with all medical procedures there was, of course, an element of risk, but I had concocted a story that was of no use to anyone. This kind of thinking was, and still is, a huge waste of my energy – energy I should be focusing on making things as good as they can be. To do this, I need to take a page out of my parents' book. It is their attitude and pragmatic approach that inspires me to examine my mindset and identify strategies to keep my thinking in check and move forwards with confidence.

* * *

At the pre-op appointment, the surgeon helpfully asked Mum what her goal was. She replied, "I want to be able to walk my little dog along Clacton seafront."

He said that he thought that was "an excellent thing to aim for," and he jokingly added he would do his best to "make sure both her legs are the same length, so you can, indeed, walk your dog along the prom."

At this point it's useful to mention that although this was a great goal to aim for, my parents didn't actually have a dog. However, the question was useful because it enabled her to identify, in a tangible way, what good would look like from her perspective. It also enabled us as a family to have an anchor in the future to refer to whenever she struggled to understand what was happening, and more importantly why it was happening. This was an achievable goal that would mark success, even though, as I say, there was no dog to walk. Maybe we could borrow one?

Hips are replaced one at a time, usually with about a year between each one. As we brought Mum home from hospital following the first operation, we were silently contemplating what the future may look like – she had really struggled to get in the car and was feeling sick and very agitated. Nothing was right, and things felt bleak. Reality had really slapped all of us in the face. The journey home was awful; Mum was so angry that we just drove in silence, a first for my family. She didn't even mention the landmark windmill, which, although a small detail, indicated to me that things were not as they should be.

Amazingly, to make things a little easier, while she was in hospital Dad had put a downstairs toilet in their house, but how would she get up to bed? Would we need to convert the lounge into a bedroom? How would Dad cope? After all, I lived 120 miles away.

When we arrived home, Mum slowly walked in using a frame. Then she said she needed the toilet, and before we could do anything or even show her the new facility, her determination kicked in and she made her way up the stairs! She wasn't without pain, but she was on a mission, and that was to prove that she wouldn't let major surgery get the better of her.

At first, we put her feelings of sickness and anger down to a mysterious and sinister after-effect of the procedure, something we couldn't do anything about. But when I phoned Simon to give him an update, ever calm and logical, he said that it was probably stomach acid and we should give her some antacid – this we did, and within a few minutes she was in a much better place, her feelings of anger slowly turning into those of pride. Before the day was done, she was telling us stories of her stay in hospital, which, as they were repeated, grew in detail, creative thinking, and entertainment value.

Despite my initial concerns and negative assumptions, both surgeries were a great success. Not only were her hips now pain-free but, due to her religiously following her exercise programme, her mobility was increasing, as was her independence. I do wonder if in a strange way her dementia assisted her recovery. She often forgot that she had had any surgery and consequently would walk around the house and up the stairs without any of that *unconscious protecting the area* that we all tend to do with injuries and the like. She was literally listening to her body, and if her body didn't tell her it was fragile, then she just got on with using it as normal.

As it turned out, the benefits of two new hips were much wider-reaching than we had imagined possible. Not only had Mum regained her physical independence, but she was also benefitting from a newfound confidence and sense of identity. This was the result of the huge amount of positive feedback and praise she was receiving. Feedback about how well she looked (being pain-free had knocked ten years off her). Feedback about her brave decision to have the surgery, and feedback about her dedication to becoming mobile and achieving her goal. The importance of this ongoing validating praise cannot be underestimated. We all benefit from being recognised for who we are and what we have achieved, and people living with dementia need it more than most of us.

Following the surgery, my mum's experience of interactions with other people completely changed. Rather than having an identity dominated by her dementia and associated symptoms, where people seemed to look out for anything *out of the ordinary* that might indicate her illness was advancing, she was now seen as the strong, courageous, driven woman she had never stopped being. Renee Batterbury had re-established her self-belief, and this spark of confidence was bright enough to make people see her for who she was, as opposed to a walking illness.

This was a big lesson for us as a family and as her support network. It confirmed for us the value and potential benefits of taking a strengths-based approach to supporting and communicating with her or any person living with dementia – in fact to anybody at all. Focus on what is working well, what they are good at, and the unique qualities they carry with them. There is a basic human need for positive affirmation, and it is all our responsibility to provide this to each other.

Hip replacements mark one of the major milestones in my mum's story, and I am happy to say that the positive long-term benefits far outweighed any short-term negative challenges. This was a classic example of my underestimation of the strength, courage, and ambition of both of my parents.

* * *

A few days before they came down to celebrate Mum's eightieth, I phoned home to finalise details of their visit. As often happens, my mum answered the telephone. "Hello?" I heard a slight stammer and sensed she was feeling a little unconfident.

"Hello Mum, it's Marcus, your favourite son!" This gave her all the information she needed and put her at ease. The *favourite son* is something both myself and my brother Martin say to her – it always makes her laugh. She humours us both with a conspiratorial hushed tone. "It's true you are my favourite."

We launched into a conversation about what we've both been up to. I told her about falling off my bike in front of a load of people on the seafront – she laughed as I shared my embarrassment, and then, seeing a link, she told me about a similar experience when, against her mum's wishes, her dad was teaching her to ride a bike all those years ago – for a few minutes we enjoyed exploring our common experience of finding freedom on two wheels, then becoming overconfident and crashing out.

Then, changing the subject, she mentioned that she had been popping next door and taking care of their neighbour Dave, making him a sandwich and a cup of tea, as he had not been well. For a moment I wondered if what she was saying was factual. Does it even matter? Not at all.

I asked her risk-free, informative, and open questions:

"Are you enjoying the sunshine?" "How are those new hips treating you?"

She was feeling very good about her hips and was clearly proud of herself for going through with the surgery, so it's good to remind her about that. She told me she had been doing her exercises every day and can walk further and further as she recovers. Getting into her stride, she also reported that she had bumped into her surgeon along the seafront, who told her he was really pleased with her progress, saying, "I wish all of my patients did as well as you – Renee." I am impressed. Then she repeated the story several times, finally adding an embellishment, "In fact, the doctor told me I had lovely legs."

Once we had caught up, I asked to speak to Dad, but her response took me by surprise. "He's not here at the moment – he's out walking the dog." I was taken aback because the truth was that they didn't have a dog – in fact, they haven't had one for about ten years. Mum clearly thought they still had their little dog, Oscar. She had forgotten he died so long ago, which is surprising because his sad demise was a memory that, up until now, she had retained and was emotive for her.

On hearing the comment, the familiar tiny fist of dread, once again, sparked in my chest – this was a new thing. Had her illness advanced to a place where she had forgotten Oscar had died, and was now imagining my dad is out walking him? Was the scope of her memory loss slowly broadening and expanding to take away more and more memories? Should I be concerned?

There was a risk of these imagined and terrible futures getting out of hand. They did not actually exist, as usual; they were just invented by me, in my head, and were based on one or two random comments made when she couldn't quite remember where her husband was. This was confirmed later when I spoke to my dad. He mentioned that he had popped out to the shop, and of course he made no reference to a dog – and neither did I. The dog comment was just a slip of the tongue and nothing to be concerned about.

A few days later, my parents pulled up in their car, and as I opened the door a small Jack Russel named Ronnie ran into our house.

"Surprise!" said my dad.

"We've had him for about a week, but we decided we would keep it a secret and swore we wouldn't tell you two until we got here!"

My lovely dad decided to help Mum achieve her goal by getting her a little rescue dog to walk along Clacton seafront. So, all my assumptions were wrong – Mum hadn't imagined the fact they had a new member of the family – she'd just forgotten it was supposed to be a secret...or better still, maybe she had remembered the secret but had decided to tell me anyway – I hope that was the case. What was my dad thinking? Like me, my mum is rubbish at keeping a secret. In fact, it's a red flag to a bull. Never tell either of us a secret...unless you want it leaked.

The arrival of Ronnie has had a huge impact on family life. Every day has an additional purpose, every walk is a necessity, both for the dog and the hips. Ronnie enjoys the enormous amount of fuss and attention he receives – he really landed on his feet by moving to Clacton – and of course, dogs attract people, so there is an extra bonus of social interactions and conversations with new people. These conversations are focused on pets – so they are risk-free, and there is little chance of *getting it wrong*. Mum grabs these opportunities to speak to other people with arms open and is usually the person who initiates chats with strangers. For somebody who struggles every day to make sense of what is going on around her, this is impressive; I think it's the spontaneity and randomness that give her confidence.

So, maybe there is a silver lining to the hip story after all...a little dog named Ronnie.

* * *

About ninety minutes after we waved to the ISS, we head back outside to see it, once again, pass 248 miles above our garden. None of us, apart from Simon who is a closet scientist, can quite believe that while we have been indoors eating, drinking, talking, and laughing, those astronauts have travelled right around the planet and here they are again waving back at us... Well, that's what we tell ourselves anyway. Simon takes this opportunity to try to explain to us that, being in orbit, the Space Station is constantly falling rather than flying – this all goes over our heads (no pun intended...).

Once those amazing men and women have disappeared over the horizon, my mum announces she is heading up to bed. I follow her to make sure she is OK, which of course she is. It is incredible to see how much her self-confidence has increased as a result of her getting new hips and, crucially, receiving positive recognition from other people. Another lesson learned.

As I watch her take her first small step to climb the stairs, I think of Neil Armstrong and his small step for man and giant leap for mankind.

People Are Kind

Spring 2013. Although we are all still very much riding the wave of positivity following her surgery, Mum's short-term memory struggles continue to go through waves of intensity. Sometimes obvious, and at other times virtually non-existent. But with my dad leading from the front, we have adjusted to this rhythm of peaks and troughs, doing our best when the going gets tough while trusting that things will be OK.

However, Dad has called to say that he is concerned because recently she seems to have entered a phase of sudden quick-fire deterioration. Her symptoms seem to be more intense and almost constant, resulting in an air of ongoing confusion, questioning, anxiety, and the need for reassurance. He says that this time it doesn't feel like things are going to improve; he adds that on a couple of occasions she hasn't recognised him and has even accused him of being a stranger in her house.

Realising he could really do with some support, we have cancelled our plans and driven up to Essex. It's early evening when we arrive, and deciding to go out for something to eat, the four of us are driving through the countryside to a pub and restaurant. Despite the situation, it's always good to be in Essex. When I was a youngster growing up, I really didn't appreciate the beauty of this county, but now, with its wide-open skies, flat landscapes and hazy horizons, it's one of my favourite places.

The pub overlooks the River Stour and is situated next to a ramshackle old boat yard, full of rusty hulls, half-built dreams, looming cranes, and Thames barges. We stand and take in the scene for a few minutes and see several different birds of prey patrolling the skies above the adjacent marshland. This is obviously a great place to hunt small mammals. Suddenly an owl swoops low over our heads, which, for the child in me, is a kind of magical and rare spectacle.

In the restaurant I am sitting opposite Mum, while Simon is talking to Dad about his dream of sailing around the world. Listening to this, I confide in her that I am hoping it's going to be a solo expedition as I would be a miserable shipmate. Cramped conditions, high seas, feeling sick and no escape. The poor man would have a nightmare just trying to deal with me, let alone coping with the Southern Ocean.

Continuing with the nautical theme, the two of us go on to talk about the canoe that Dad bought me and Martin when we were kids. This was a top present because we lived next to a river, and having a boat meant we could go on adventures – not together obviously, because we couldn't stand the sight of each other, but we could paddle off separately with our own friends. The only problem was that the canoe was old, was made of perishing canvas, and had a substantial leak. Considering this, and with health and safety always at the forefront of his mind, Dad also gave us a saucepan, as constant baling out was required to keep our boat of dreams afloat.

Mum is laughing as I talk about this, but then she gets serious with a vague look of confusion and she says, "You are not my son, are you... You're too big."

This is not even a question; it's a statement. I realise that although I am familiar to her, at this point she is unsure who I am. Simon and Dad are still talking boats and haven't heard our conversation. Despite the mild shockwave that travels through my body, I try to respond in a light-hearted way and tell her that I am her son and the reason I'm so big is because I'm now in my forties.

She laughs, and then turning serious again says, "You are daft... You're not really my son, though, are you." Again, this is a statement.

Then she looks into my eyes and asks, "What is your name?"

I remind her of my name and ask her where it came from; Marcus was not a common name – what made her choose it for me? This question builds a bridge of connection between us, and eventually she starts to believe me, but for a short time I can sense a wariness.... *Is this man lying to me?*

I play it down and make no fuss, and after an uneasy few minutes we are back to being mother and son. Our other halves are not aware of what has just happened, and neither of us say anything; to be honest, I think Mum may have already forgotten. This is the first time she has not recognised who I am in relation to her. It's one of those things you hear about when people talk about dementia, but luckily for us on this occasion, as with the two previous times with my dad, it is so short-lived that by the time it has sunk in it is already in the past. But I can't escape the fact that this is new and is a sign that, as my dad has said, things are moving on, and maybe in the future this may be far more common or even permanent.

As the four of us enjoy a few post-dinner drinks, the continuously sinking canoe comes into the conversation again. The joyful punchline to this story is that one night somebody stole it. This was of course upsetting and not joyful at the time, but the hilarious silver lining to this sad tale was that the thief didn't take the saucepan. We estimated that his speedy getaway was thwarted after about twenty minutes as his vessel would have, no doubt, sunk. Simon is looking at the three of us laughing into our glasses and is wondering how he ever got tangled up with us in the first place.

* * *

The next evening after Mum has taken herself to bed, Dad shares that sometimes he worries about what other people think or how they might react to her. Will they ridicule or be cruel to her? Which would be just unbearable. Will they patronise or infantilise her? Or, worse still, will they just plain ignore her? In sharing these concerns, he is coming from a place of love and protection – he wants to keep his lovely wife safe. When he speaks about this, I realise that inside I have been having the same thoughts, and the incident in the restaurant has added to my concerns. The difference is that unlike my dad, once again, I have not been brave enough to admit it, even to myself.

This is a topic that is difficult for us to talk about – it feels a little deceitful, but if we can't explore it with each other, who can we speak to?

Simon is a rock; he makes it OK and normal for us to have these feelings. It's like being given permission to be honest, even if it doesn't feel right. He then says something that is incredibly helpful, and which both myself and my dad grab hold of with both hands.

He says, "If you want Mum to live her best life, you must trust that *all* people are kind. If you allow yourselves to think otherwise and try to protect her by keeping her away from people, the only person to really suffer would be her."

He knows Mum very well, and he knows what a social animal she is. She speaks to people, she loves babies, kids, and dogs, and wants to connect with them and their parents, brothers, sisters and, in the case of the dogs, their owners. These random but regular interactions are a joy to her. They provide her with an enormous sense of wellbeing and value and, as I have said before, this is where the magic happens.

Although he acknowledges the risks associated with being around other people, Simon also gets us to think about the potential effect on her welfare if she is kept away from them. The benefits far outweigh any risks – either real or imagined.

My dad and I take his comments on board. It's like seeing the light for the first time, but we just needed somebody to point it out to us.

So, as well as being *with Mum in her truth and in the moment*, we are also going to *trust that all people are kind.* It's simple but feels liberating and strangely empowering.

Beach Huts and Cabins

It's 2014, Simon and I are once again in Essex with my parents and, other than having a catch up, this visit has an additional purpose. We are here to look at some small wooden buildings in a place called Wrabness. We are designing a wooden cabin to be built at the end of our garden in Sussex and we are looking for ideas. I use the word *designing* liberally. I'm talking biro on graph paper with estimated measurements – it's literally a *back-of-a-fag-packet* sort of affair, and we are loving it.

Like the pub and boatyard we visited last year, Wrabness sits on the south shore of the River Stour. From the beach there are views across the estuary towards Suffolk, and the giant cranes of Harwich and Felixstowe, which look like a scene from *War of the Worlds*. Wrabness Beach has something of New Zealand about it. It has the air of being of another time and another place – not the sort of beach I would imagine could be found in England.

Sitting up high on stilts and ledges close to the water's edge is the row of spectacular little huts and cabins we have come to see. I came here years ago, and it struck me then as the kind of spot I would like to live in, and my memory serves me well – because it certainly is. The buildings are a hotchpotch of creativity with no apparent rules. The main building materials seem to be pitch-black wood and corrugated tin. Each structure is unique and interesting, but together they become something quite magical.

This place would make a great setting for a music video – in my head I am playing "Weightless Again" by The Handsome Family – my eyes become the camera, and scan across this strange land- and waterscape as the music and lyrics add a sepia wash.

* * *

The little row of random buildings certainly provides Simon and I with an injection of inspiration and confidence, so we take some photos and get excited about our fag packet project.

The only noticeable difference between now and when I first visited Wrabness is a new sign saying *Private Beach*; a sad and telling addition to such a wild and beautiful landscape. It's amazing how two words can taint my view of a place if I let it – which I do not. Treating this addition with the respect it deserves, we take a walk along the beach.

Immersing myself in the *cabin life*, I am now describing one I stayed in for a few weeks on Waiheke Island near Auckland. It sat on stilts above a small, quiet beach. It had a little wooden rowing boat, a snorkel and mask, and some fishing tackle stashed underneath it. Hanging on a tree to the right of the door was a homemade mobile, constructed out of fishing line, driftwood, and odd pieces of flotsam and jetsam that had been collected by beachcombers. I added to this by finding and attaching a well-travelled piece of blue plastic rope with a crab claw hanging on to it for dear life – it was so desperate to stay connected that it just didn't realise its body was missing. Opposite the door, on the beach, there were two old wooden chairs, and a fire pit made from a rusty oil drum. I had some good books, some swimming trunks, a pair of running shoes and an overwhelming feeling of freedom and contentment – a rare and valuable feeling.

This is just one of the many cabin-related experiences that have made me feel that way and have, for some reason, shaped my idea of what a good life looks like. Whether it be the chalets of Jaywick, the long-legged beach huts of Frinton, Prospect Cottage in Dungeness, or a shack constructed out of old bookcases and wiggly tin in a Queensland rain forest – they have all informed my belief that I will probably end up, as an old, grey, hairy bloke, sitting in a cabin, looking out at the world and grinning – although, due to his obsession with very nice record players and audio equipment, Simon may have something to say about this. It's certainly something we need to take in to account when building our own cabin at the end of the garden. I'm looking for the wild woods and pugs, while he is looking for pre-amps and subwoofers.

* * *

When we have taken our photographs and reached the end of the beach, rather than go back the way we came, we decide to climb up a steep bank into a wooded area in search of our next port of call, a pub that serves lunch. As we trudge about trying to get our bearings, it becomes apparent that what started as a gentle dog walk has become quite the adventure. I am so amazed by the real, tangible difference my mum's new hips are making. They have given her a new lease of life. I know her goal was to walk her little dog along Clacton seafront, but clambering over logs and stiles, as well as through spikey undergrowth, is a whole different ball game.

I compliment her on her off-road abilities, which are truly impressive. As always, this positive encouragement gives her a boost – she is now on even more of a mission to prove what she is capable of. As we continue our hike, she is in good spirits, joining in with the banter and taking part in the conversation – of which she is now taking full control, telling us about the spooky woods she and her sister played in behind number 1 Parker Avenue many years ago.

Simon spots a rope swing with a tyre on the end hanging

from a high bough over the water. While we stand and watch him swing, Mum asks me where we are going and why, she then goes on to ask what day it is and are we going to have lunch or have we already had it. She isn't asking these questions from a place of anxiety or worry – she is just looking for clarity. It's interesting that despite her mild confusion, she is having an enjoyable experience right now in the moment, being a part of the action along with everybody else. It occurs to me that the combination of chatting and laughing with people that love and respect her and taking part in a nice walk that will conclude with a pub lunch kind of outweighs any negatives associated with not being able to remember the practical details of what we are doing and why. This makes perfect sense – she is focusing on the important things in life – lunch, laughter, and love.

* * *

Later that day, and after visiting Grayson Perry's *House for Essex*, we are back at my parents' home. I know that over the last year or two, Mum has become increasingly dubious about visitors coming to stay – even close family. On our last visit I asked Dad if this was still the case, and unfortunately it was. This realisation had a sobering effect on us. We visit my parents, or they visit us regularly with the aim of hopefully giving them a sense of being part of a wider family who care about them, while also enabling them to feel supported and less isolated. But actually, in doing so, we are at risk of unintentionally exacerbating the problems they experience.

This is quite a complex issue that is difficult to manage positively. Once Mum knows we, or any other visitors, are coming, she will usually go through a period of excitement about seeing people who are important to her and having somebody other than my dad to talk to. But she will then become preoccupied with the details, which are usually focused on other people's expectations of her. Where will they sleep? Are the beds clean? Will they need feeding? How long are they staying? This worry then becomes the central theme and kind of overshadows any of the initial excitement. In fact, due to her short-term memory issues, she will often forget who is coming but will retain the feelings of threat and risk, and this is not good for her or my dad's welfare.

However, now he tells me that this time things have been much better. He has introduced a couple of simple ideas that seem to have eased her concerns. The first is that he didn't tell her we were coming until the morning of our arrival. Now it all makes sense! I wondered why he sent a text asking me not to say anything about our visit to her on the phone. I just went with it without really thinking or asking why. This sounds a little extreme but, as he says, once we are here, she absolutely loves being with us in the moment. What he has done is remove the period of angst in the build-up to the visit. I think about our overseas visitors all those years ago. The build-up was appalling, but the actual event was comparatively smooth sailing. If only they really had "turned up out of the blue," as Mum continues to say they did.

Recognising her increased need for information and details, the second thing he has done is attach a *write-on, wipe-off* whiteboard to the kitchen wall alongside the calendar and the clock. Deciding to take advantage of the fact she visits this area of the kitchen as a first port of call whenever she needs questions answered, he thought this may well help. I go into the kitchen and check it out. When we arrived this morning and took our gear upstairs, with Dad's support Mum wrote all the information she needed on the whiteboard:

Marcus and Simon arrived on Saturday; they leave on Monday morning.

We are going out for a pub lunch both days and having fish and chips in the evening.

Later in our stay, more information appears:

Simon and Marcus will do their own laundry when they get home.

This was obviously in response to some kind of concern that had come to light.

A little later I notice:

Simon and Marcus love Renee very much xxxx.

has appeared in Simon's handwriting.

Of course, these simple steps do not entirely solve the issues, but they do help. She still asks loads of questions, which we are all happy to answer. But on Sunday morning when we are sitting in the lounge chatting, I do notice her become a little preoccupied. She is looking at the clock, checking her watch and looking to see if the table is set for a meal. I can almost imagine her asking herself, "Are they expecting me to feed them?" – but before I can intervene, she gets up and makes her way into the kitchen, probably to check if anything is cooking – five minutes later, having clearly looked at the whiteboard, she comes back into the lounge and interrupts the morning conversation by announcing she is taking us out for lunch at the pub and she is paying! This is received as a great idea by all and is followed by much hilarity due to comments about moths flying out of her purse, etc.

Driving home the next day, Simon and I are once again discussing my dad's pragmatic and logical approach to enabling his wife to bypass her worries as much as possible and retain her sense of independence and her role within our family.

This is truly inspiring stuff...simple and effective.

We are also talking excitedly about our plans to build a cabin at the end of the garden!

Finding Jessie

Our small green campervan has provided us with perfect transport and accommodation on all our holidays since we bought it twenty years ago. It's summer 2016, and today we are leading the way in a two-vehicle convoy, heading west along the south coast of England – our destination Exmouth, and Jessie.

The soundtrack in the van today is dominated by Paul Simon's *Graceland*, David Bowie's *Hunky Dory*, and Talking Heads' *Stop Making Sense* – three of our favourite road trip albums, which we do our best to sing along with as we make our way along the M27 at a pace that can only feel fast in a 1976 VW Camper.

Looking in the wing mirror, I can see Mum and Dad behind us in their silver car. Every now and again we lose them and pull into a lay-by to allow them to catch up. This stretch of road is particularly beautiful, taking us through the New Forest, one of our favourite places to go camping, cycling, and walking.

The New Forest was established in 1079 by William the Conqueror, who took ownership of the land and made it his own hunting ground. That's all very nice, but in doing so he also banned common folk from using the land for grazing their livestock or foraging for food and fuel. I imagine this would have had a significant bearing on the health and livelihood of all those families and communities who, up until that point, had lived off the land – and all for the sake of a good day's hunting for those further up the power ladder. Luckily, almost one thousand years later, the New Forest is now a National Park, open to all and used by the local community.

The landscape of the forest is a combination of ancient woodlands and open heathland, populated by an awe-inspiring combination of flora and fauna. In the woods, the ground is covered in a blanket of moss, ferns, fallen trees and spectacular fungi. The heath is dominated by dry earth, gorse, grasses and, if you are lucky, spongy bogs and sundews.

There is a large population of deer and wild ponies that roam freely and help themselves to whatever is on offer, or not. The ponies are particularly adept at literally raiding tents and taking anything edible they can lay their hooves on. The deer spend most of their time hidden and foraging in the woods, but when they do occasionally appear they are silent, curious, and alert. A few seconds of eye contact with a majestic buck or doe while it checks you out before disappearing is a wonderful thing that everybody should experience. Meanwhile, high above the wood and heathland, the skies are patrolled by buzzards and kestrels during the day, and as night falls, bats and owls take over as top airborne predators.

Despite this abundance of wildlife, by far our favourite creatures in the forest are the southern wood ants. These incredible little creatures march around the coniferous woodland in single file, either collecting pine needles, twigs, and leaves to build their huge and fabulous nests, or hunting various invertebrates to feed the community. Each nest can accommodate up to half a million ants, and there are hundreds if not thousands of nests in the New Forest. Simon and I, being creatures of habit ourselves, have one particular nest we visit each year – we call this our pilgrimage to the Ant Hill Mob.

However, although it is wonderful to be driving our green and beautiful van through this green and beautiful land, we will not be visiting any ants or sundews today; instead, we will be passing straight through the forest and heading for

Lulworth Cove on the Jurassic Coast of Dorset.

As we continue our journey, I look over my shoulder into the back of the van to make sure Milo is OK. He is laying in what can only be described as a ridiculously uncomfortable position. Legs akimbo, with his bottom higher than his head, but he is snoring as only a pug can. He has a contented and crooked grin on his face, with one eye slightly open, so I guess all is good with him.

Through the back window I can see that Mum, Dad and Ronnie are still following. They are close enough for me to recognise my mum's distinctive head movements telling me that she is speaking. I'm pretty sure she will be enjoying the journey. I imagine she will be giving my dad and the dog a running commentary on what she is seeing, which will include cars, caravans, cyclists, ponies and of course us in our campervan. I wave to her, but she doesn't see me. Like all car journeys, as well as reading road signs and sharing her observations with my dad, she will be regularly asking where they are heading and why. My dad will be reassuring her that everything is organised, and she hasn't got anything to worry about, and crucially this holiday was all her idea. We are going to find Jessie!

* * *

This whole road trip came into being as a direct result of my dad's ongoing and spirited refusal to let his age dictate how he lives his life. He has a strong aversion to being categorised or stereotyped according to his years, and he will not be penned in and restricted by other people's assumptions. In fact, rather than being limiting, these assumptions act as a red flag, and he will go out of his way to prove them wrong. I guess this is a quality he and his wife have in common.

This ambition is particularly evident when it comes to harnessing new technology. Being a curious man with a keenness to gain new skills, he approaches this with an unwavering tenacity and willingness to learn from his mistakes. In light of this, and the fact that his PC was so slow it drove him crackers, we decided to all chip in and buy him an iPad for his birthday. For a family with a rich history of buying unsuccessful and, at times, nonsensical gifts for each other, I must say that on this occasion we got it right!

He was over the moon with his new gadget and pleased that we saw him as a man who embraces digital innovation, which he is. To witness my dad's determination to overcome obstacles and make new technology a part of his life is impressive, as he does not find it easy. In fact, he seems to find it both fascinating and frustrating in equal measures. But he usually nails it eventually, and getting to grips with the iPad was no different.

Within weeks he was on social media, was streaming music, and was even doing his banking and shopping on-line. Which, for a man who has an inbuilt suspicion of everyone on the planet, was a remarkable achievement. Crucially, in addition to this he introduced the magic of the internet to his wife, and with his support it has gone on to provide her with feelings of connection, increased self-confidence, and even a sense of belonging. Whether they are listening to Nat King Cole, searching out significant and familiar places, or watching videos of particular events, the internet brings memories to life, and in doing so, reaffirms her place in the world and pride in who she is.

A few weeks after the arrival of the new gadget, we were all having dinner together, and as is often the case, Mum was holding court, this time telling us an often-repeated story about her dad's friendship with John 'Cat's Eyes' Cunningham. After the war John had gone on to be a test pilot and famously flew the world's first jet airliner – the De Havilland Comet. Ted had continued to be his driver and took great pride in knowing this *brave man of the skies* (as Mum described him). While she was adding bells and whistles to this story, my dad and Simon used the iPad to find a newsreel of John coming down the steps of the Comet and being interviewed by the world's press. They then played this for Mum through the TV – tears ran down her face as this almost mythical man from the past was brought back to life along with her lovely dad. Proof, if any is needed, of how technology can be used to open doors and make connections across distance, time, and generations.

The internet has also enabled them to track down long-lost friends, and Jessie and Roy were at the top of the *must find* list. It turned out that Jessie was a social media fiend herself, so it wasn't long before they had linked up and were rekindling their friendship. This connection resulted in the emergence of many long forgotten memories, and Mum soon made it clear that she really wanted to meet up with Jessie, in person. We grabbed hold of this suggestion with both hands, because since her dementia has taken hold, she very rarely, if ever, suggests doing anything out of the ordinary, preferring instead to stay in a familiar environment with predictable routines, which of course makes perfect sense if you think about it.

* * *

As we ate breakfast this morning, there was a real atmosphere of excitement. Mum was telling stories about she and Jessie sewing goggles to earn a few pounds while their kids were too young for school, the two of them going out in the car once Mum had passed her driving test, and the two couples taking their kids for days out to the seaside with buckets, spades, toy boats and flags all crammed into the tiny boot of the car. As she spoke, she had an air of ownership – as if Simon, Dad and I were just coming along for the ride. This is a rare thing and is always good to see – life is interesting when she makes the rules!

Seeing an opportunity, I shared my own memory of those days, when I overheard a conversation between Jessie and Mum saying that Roy had always wanted a son and Mum and Dad had wanted a daughter. This conversation included a joke about swapping one of each, which my young ears took very, very seriously. On hearing this I became intensely suspicious that they were hatching a dark plan to trade offspring, and hope that nobody would notice. My suspicions all came to a head a few weeks later when Mum and I bumped into Jessie and her youngest daughter, Jackie, at the swings and slide in the local playing field. I was convinced this meeting was no coincidence and was in fact a pre-arranged child swap. My only option was to behave in a way that would leave Jessie with very little doubt that she was better off with Jackie, and that Renee and Guy would just have to keep me and get over it.

Of course, being my mother's son, I elaborated and exaggerated this story. It was worth it, though, as Mum couldn't stop laughing and was now adding her own details to give my tale some kick. She said she remembered me refusing to go down the slide in case I was grabbed and kidnapped at the bottom, and that I refused to speak to Jackie in case she was in on the plan. Eventually we headed back down the high street, myself with Mum, and Jackie with Jessie, and I never overheard child swaps mentioned again.

As we told this story, handing it back and forth to each other for extra details, Dad and Simon both looked bemused, not knowing whether to believe us or not. One of the many things I love about my mum is that she is always willing to contribute to other people's truths, bringing them to life and making them real. This has nothing to do with her dementia; she just likes to tell a good tale. I appreciate this because, in relation to the *child swap incident*, I have no idea what actually happened and what was in my head, and I'm pretty sure that at the time of telling, we both knew that very little of what we were saying was likely to be true. But of course, it doesn't matter; it's making us laugh.

* * *

Despite the respite that this little trip into the past provided, the truth is that the journey we are embarking on today is out of the ordinary; nothing about it is that predictable or familiar, and as we finished our breakfast Mum suddenly went from being in control of this whole trip and directing the packing to a place of confusion and not wanting to go at all. It's like the conversation we had just been having totally disappeared from her memory bank.

Then there was an almost angry barrage of questions.

"Where are we going? Who will be there? When is this happening? Why are we doing this?" And, crucially, "What is expected of me?"

Before we knew it, we had fallen into a spiral of repeated questions, answers and building frustration.

Then my dad stood up looked at his wife and assertively said, "We are going to Exmouth to see Jessie because she was one of your best friends; it was all your idea, and there's nothing to worry about!"

He then added, "Now, who wants a cup of tea?"

Silence.

And like the magnetic poles, things reversed.

"Of course! I can't wait to see Jessie, I'll make the tea, you sit down." And she headed into the kitchen. As she did this, Simon put Johnny Mathis on CD player.

This approach to supporting Mum to navigate through her confusion and to find a place of confidence and security isn't an exact science, to be frank; it doesn't always work. Sometimes her concerns will take up so much space that there really isn't any room left to process fresh information, and the cycle of questions, and our well-intended answers, just frustrates her. When this happens, this morning being a good example, we try to change the subject and redirect her attention to something completely different. If this sounds complicated, you will be pleased to know that it isn't; it usually involves somebody saying something like "Who fancies a cup of tea?" "Whose turn is it to wash the dishes?" or "Does the dog need a walk around the block?"

When these kinds of questions are asked, Mum will invariably jump up and step into what she sees as her role in our family – once again she confirms her identity and feelings of value.

This morning the subject was changed by my dad suggesting a cup of tea, which also involved a change of environment – going into the kitchen to put the kettle on. And all of this was enhanced by the introduction of Mr. Mathis, a reliable anchor for many stories and conversations.

* * *

Eventually we arrive in Lulworth Cove, where we have a two-night stopover before we head for Exmouth. Lulworth is a place that we visited as a family when Martin and I were kids. My memory tells me that this was the first time I had stayed in a caravan, and I loved it. All the mad little gadgets and bits of furniture that changed their use depending on the time of day. Tables became headboards and sofas turned into beds. There was a mild smell of mildew and gas, and the floor creaked as we walked around. To add to the appeal and excitement, my dad was convinced that a mouse was in residence – in light of this, both me and Mum put down little secret stashes of biscuit crumbs for his supper.

This was my kind of home. Maybe one day I could live in a caravan, and if I didn't like the neighbours, I could just get somebody to tow me somewhere new. Why have a house that's stuck in one place if you can have one on wheels? This was a revelation to me, and it is wonderful to be back here as a grownup in my own house on wheels.

Mum, Dad, and Ronnie are staying in a pub in the village centre, while Simon, Milo and I are staying nearby in a campsite with caravans. I wonder if this is where we stayed in the early seventies. My dad confirms that it is.

The Jurassic coastline is spectacular and has been classified as a world heritage site, with prehistoric evidence of dinosaurs, including footprints, fossils, and fantastic rock strata spanning back millions of years. The campsite is up high on a steep hill above Durdle Door, a natural limestone arch that is slowly, but constantly, reshaped by the sea.

Close by, there is a military zone that is used for training by the Ministry of Defence. As it gets dark, we can hear gun shots and are surprised to see tracer fire drawing trails up high across the night sky. This is such a strange paradoxical experience. Simon, Milo and I are sitting around our fire bucket in this wild, peaceful and ancient landscape, while at the same time we are watching and hearing war games taking place high above our heads in the crystal dark starry night. We are so lucky to be living a life where gunfire and trails in the sky is a surprising and intriguing phenomenon, as opposed to being life-threatening and fear-inducing.

The next morning, we are all sitting in a café, and Simon is talking about the unexpected spectacle we had witnessed the previous evening. Dad goes on to tell us about the V2 Rockets that rained down on the UK during the war, and a particular rocket that screamed its way over the rooftops of Roydon and exploded at the other end of the village.

* * *

It was Christmas and like with every other year since the conflict began, there was an informal agreement that there would be no fighting. At this time there was an older man living with Dad's family. He was an evacuee from the East End of London. Because of the festive season, his daughter and grandchildren, who were also evacuated and staying with another local family, were visiting and everybody was crammed into the small lounge along with Dad and his two brothers. My dad's mum, Iris, had just left the house with a bag of Guinness bottles she had hidden in the garden. She was on her way down to the pub to get the money back on the empties and maybe use it to buy a couple of full ones.

Suddenly there was a deafening screaming noise and then a huge explosion. The house shook and the windows were all blown out, as were the shop fronts in the high street. Just like the first significant bomb in Bengeo, after the dust had settled, there was an eerie silence. Then in the distance a faint rattling sound and slightly alarming running footsteps. My dad and his brothers instantly panicked, thinking the Germans had landed and they were all going to be taken prisoner – the panic was infectious and soon spread to the family of evacuees. As the sound of footsteps got closer, everybody sat in hushed silence hoping they would go past. But they stopped outside the house, and the noise changed to jangling keys, rattling bottles and Iris swearing about Hitler!

Dad's telling of this story is very funny, and I can just imagine my tiny little nan running up the road terrified, in her housecoat, with a fag on and a load of empties in a carrier bag. He rarely shares stories from the past, particularly about the war, and when he does, it reminds me that as children my parents only lived about nine miles apart, both of them living under the same threatening skies.

After coffee we wander down to the little bay of Lulworth Cove and take photographs. There is one that I particularly love. It's of Simon and Mum sitting on the sea wall with their arms over each other's shoulders, pulling funny faces and smiling at the camera. This picture perfectly captures their unique, loving, and conspiratorial relationship. It has always struck me as something more than just a bond between a woman and her son's life partner.

* * *

The next day we are sitting in a pub garden in Exmouth eating lunch with Roy and Jessie. It's wonderful to see them. Despite the forty-year gap, they all pick up where they had left off, chatting, laughing and telling their stories. Once we've eaten, Simon and I walk the dogs along the seafront and leave the four old friends to it for a while.

Spending a couple of days with them is a tonic for all of us. They are truly great people and have welcomed us with open arms. It would have been so much easier not to head West to see them in person. We could have just had a few phone conversations, and the odd email, but within ten minutes of meeting up it is clear that the whole trip has been worthwhile. Mum and Jessie are reminiscing about goggling, and Roy and Dad are talking about years ago when we went out to sea off Plymouth in Roy's little fishing boat.

In the weeks that follow our road trip, my mum is on a high. Feeling that she planned something that benefited everybody. Sometimes she remembers what we did and other times she doesn't, but she continues to carry the enormous sense of accomplishment, and emotional wellbeing, that she experienced meeting up with her dear friends, and this is a great thing to see.

Greek Gods and Apollo Wives

It is autumn 2016, and it's been a few months since our visit to Exmouth. After a spell of plateauing, Mum's condition seems to have subtly progressed, and this time it is not only linked to her deteriorating ability to retain new information, but also to her perception of her appearance, and this, once again, is a new thing. Dad has been telling me about it on the phone over the last few weeks, so I have driven up to stay for a couple of days – something I should do far more regularly than I do.

I know that he finds it frustrating that he will tell me and Simon about issues that are worrying him, and then when we get together, Mum is so busy proving how well she's doing that these concerns are not so obvious. It makes him feel as though he is making a fuss about nothing, which isn't the case at all. It is vital that he can air his thoughts and concerns, be heard and taken seriously. But I know I get a different version of Mum to the one that he sees daily. If you think about it, we all behave slightly differently depending on who we are with, and where we are, and my mum is no different. When she is with Simon and me, it's like she is on high alert and keen to demonstrate her independence and achievements. It feels as if she has something to prove – the great thing about this is that we can then pile on the positive feedback, which, of course makes her feel good about herself. But sometimes this is at the detriment of us getting a deeper picture of how she is really doing. That is why it is so important for my dad to share his views and perceptions. However, in this case, the changes he has described are plain to see.

* * *

For as far back as I can remember, every morning Mum has religiously gone through the motions of choosing her clothes, getting dressed, looking in the mirror, checking her appearance and adding a bit of lipstick and powder. Of course, more recently, throughout the day, drinks get spilt, dog paws dab little footprints, clothes become dishevelled and lippy gets smudged and reapplied. But today things are different; she is looking in the mirror, but she doesn't seem to be taking in, or processing, what she is seeing. It's as if she is looking at her reflection because that is all part of the routine, but she is not sure what she is looking for. So, this morning she came downstairs with large and obvious dark coffee stains on her pale pink cardigan and trousers, and her hair had clearly not been touched. Apparently, this is the third or fourth time this has happened in the past week or so.

On the face of it, neither of these issues is really that important. The world won't end, we are not going anywhere or expecting any visitors, so what does it matter? In fact, when I take a moment to think about what I look like this morning – unwashed, unshaven, odd socks and shorts that are just a tad too short – I really can't pass judgement on anybody else. So, what's the problem? Well, in truth there isn't one, but the reason this is so noticeable is that it is totally out of character for a woman who prides herself on her appearance and will regularly spend a great deal of time making sure she's looking her best. After we have eaten breakfast, she goes back to the full-length mirror and once again does not see the stains or comb her hair. A while later she is in front of the mirror again, this time for about ten minutes, I can hear her quietly talking to herself. It's as if she knows something is different but she can't identify what.

I don't want her to feel criticised; there is nothing worse than somebody making negative comments about your appearance – no matter how good their intentions are. I call out, "Are you OK, Mum?"

"Of course I am," she replies with an urgency, as if she has been caught.

I recognise an element of concern in her voice. I decide to suggest we get dressed up and go out for a coffee, which will help her, and I know she will ask me how she looks. But while I am thinking about this, I hear her climb back up the stairs.

A little later she appears with a comb in her hand. "I can't believe it; I forgot to put a comb through my hair this morning – whatever made me do that?"

I point out my odd socks and dodgy shorts, then I suggest going out, and the plan works. She climbs the stairs once more and comes down with clean clothes on and I do the same thing. We jokingly check each other over, I tell her she looks beautiful, she thanks me with a big smile on her face and then mentions she doesn't like my cropped hair.

An hour later we are sitting in a café people watching. I imagine they are doing the same thing – I wonder what they make of the two of us.

I notice her perfume. "You smell good."

"Do I? Thank you."

I reckon it's Chanel N°5, her favourite. I usually buy her a bottle on Mother's Day or her birthday – she loves the box and the tissue paper it's wrapped in as much as the perfume itself. Chanel, for my mum, represents that *fabulous life that other people lead* she first became aware of when her dad was a chauffeur all those years ago. Our past conversations have also taught me that, for her, there are clear links between Chanel, Jackie Kennedy, and the Apollo astronaut wives.

Having a spray of Chanel N°5 now and again does Mum

no end of good; it always has. I love the fact that just a smell can open the door to all kinds of memories, nostalgia, and good feelings.

"Is that Chanel N°5 I can smell, you fabulous woman?" I ask.

This question instantly results in a smile, and off we go into a story about her and my dad going up to London with a group of friends to attend a concert at the Festival Hall and to have a meal. All dressed up and having a lovely time. She is telling me about a handsome waiter that told her she smelt good and enquired what perfume she was wearing.

"Chanel N°5," she replied,

"Of course it is, Madame," he said with a smile. "Why would you wear anything else?"

That little interaction was the highlight of the evening, and maybe the year. I ask her who they saw in concert – she has no idea. Nice perfume and a handsome waiter had even trumped Frank or Ella.

Mum's love of Chanel reaches much further than just perfume. For as far back as I can remember she has coveted one of their handbags. This was an item that sat in an imagined glass case on a pedestal high above anything else in relation to what it represented to her. It was as if a handbag could offer a portal to an alternative life. Not that she wasn't happy and content with how things had panned out for her and my dad, but we all have the parallel lives we didn't lead, that now and again emerge into our consciousness. And for Renee Batterbury, in her parallel life, she is clutching a Chanel handbag.

I remember when I was a youngster, she and I were watching a TV programme about the Apollo space missions. At one point, as the Saturn 5 Rocket pushed the astronauts high into the darkening blue sky, the camera cut to their wives, heads tilted back, fabulous hairstyles and killer sunglasses.

As the camera panned out, a handbag appeared at the bottom of the screen, being held tightly by one of these amazing women. Mum took a quick breath in and whispered in hushed reverence,

"*Look! It's Chanel.*" She was far more awestruck by the handbag than by the men sitting in a rocket and heading into space.

She then went on to tell me that at NASA, every astronaut's wife was given a Chanel handbag. Even then, all those years ago, long before we had even heard of Alzheimer's, she was telling stories and inventing truths that, even to my naive ears, sounded dubious at best. But I bought into it anyway – and this became a kind of truth, which, in respect for my mum, I have kept with me into adulthood. To this day I see these women as the most glamorous on Earth – which they are. More recently I have noticed that astronauts' husbands are impressive too – but I think they get free watches instead – which is a shame.

* * *

Many years after the Apollo missions, I was working with my friend Emmanuel, a wonderful Greek man who had emigrated with his much-loved family from a small village in Greece to Sydney, Australia. Emmanuel spoke with a kind of knowing authority. It always seemed as if his wise words were coming from a place of deep thought and understanding, with a strong sense of right and wrong.

One day he was speaking to me about the importance of family and, particularly, wives and mothers. He said that it is our role (as husbands and sons) to do all we can to make their dreams come true. He then told me that a few weeks later his wife would be celebrating her fortieth birthday, and he had bought her something that would definitely do this for her. What a great bloke – he was so genuine and cared deeply about people, particularly his loved ones. As he was telling me this, I reflected that at that time I was working and saving money to continue travelling the world, all for my own gratuitous, and maybe selfish, benefit. My plans were all about me and nobody else. My family didn't really get a look in, other than the fact that they were there for me, and they would no doubt be my safety blanket if I needed them to be. I was embarrassed as I admitted this to myself, and I made an internal pledge that from now on, I would not take them for granted – I needed to be a bit more like Emmanuel and remember the people I loved.

Curious, I asked Emmanuel what he had bought his wife. What was it that would make her dreams come true?

"A second-hand bus," he replied in all seriousness and with great enthusiasm.

"It's in good condition and runs like a dream; I've even had her name painted down each side. She's going to be so happy!"

He went on to tell me that Sadie had always wanted to drive a school bus, and he had not only bought her the vehicle of her dreams but also secured a contract with a local school! I wasn't expecting this, and I found it wonderful, if a little surprising, as I hope she did. I never thought to ask if Sadie had a license or the ability to drive a bus – I assume she did.

I went on to tell him the story of my mum's obsession with Chanel handbags, and the fact that in some ways they signified the alternative life she hadn't led but would like a taste of.

Emmanuel's jaw dropped. "And you haven't bought her one?!" he said, incredulous.

Right then and there, he made me solemnly promise that when I got back to the UK, I would do everything I could to buy her that handbag – he said that a handbag wasn't much to ask, and getting her one was the least I could do for the woman who had given birth to me!

My Greek friend meant what he said, and he was right; I needed to buy the handbag. I held onto this advice, and about a year later I did manage to do so; it was beautiful, and she cherished it. I sent Emmanuel a postcard to say I had been inspired by Sadie's bus, and just like her, my mum was now living the dream.

* * *

Thirty years later, I am sitting in the café asking Mum about the handbag.

She tells me, “It’s in its box, wrapped in tissue, and only comes out on very special occasions.”

I don’t know if this is fact – but it works for her, and it’s working for me.

Of course, this little trip to the café and down memory lane hasn’t changed the fact that her condition seems to be slowly tightening its grip in different ways. But that doesn’t mean we can’t continue to enjoy the finer things in life – the times of joy, coffee, cakes, chats, and handbags still far outweigh any struggles we may have. Who cares about a few stains on a jacket? The deep and rich magic will still happen if we want it to...and maybe a quick spray of a certain perfume will help it on its way.

Diagnosis?

It's January 2017, and this morning I had a long email from Jessie, saying that our visit was the highlight of last year – which it was for us as well. She was impressed with how happy and healthy Mum appeared even with her obvious memory issues, and she went on to ask when Mum was diagnosed. This is a tricky subject in our household because despite our best efforts, up until now she has refused to see a doctor or have an assessment – there is no diagnosis.

Although there is a very clear trajectory for the illness, it continues to be unpredictable. She may not recognise me now, but she may well know who I am when I walk into the room in thirty minutes' time. Let's face it, we all have bad days, times when we wake in a fog, or things are on the tip of our tongue, and we just can't find the right words or phrases to say what we want to say. But the difference for you and I is, for most of our lives, people aren't monitoring everything we do or say – people are not looking for signs and confirmation that things are worsening.

In general, when changes are noticed, we rarely discuss them with her unless there is a real need, and if this is the case she will let us know. For most of the time, as she tells us regularly, she feels "fit, well, and happy." She sees any illness or injury as something quite separate to herself, something she is just putting up with until things improve, or a strategy is identified to overcome the problem.

As I have described in previous chapters, these homemade strategies come in many different guises, some practical and some behavioural, but the main principle is that they help overcome the issue in a simple and empowering way. So rather than focus our energy and attention on the actual change or problem, and in doing so make her feel potentially insecure, we take a subtle but proactive approach to identify and test drive solutions.

Although the many ways in which her illness manifests itself can at times be challenging, and even surprising, we try to keep a firm grip on the fact that she is the complete person that we love very much, who happens to be living with dementia. In a way, we are following her example of separating her from the illness; she is not Alzheimer's disease, she is Renee Batterbury – mother, wife, and friend. Thinking about this, it is also important for us to remember that many of the behaviours and habits that she displays are just a part of who she is and always has been. She has always been a little unpredictable, which is what makes her so much fun to be around, and she has never had 100% reliable memory – do any of us? And although I love her dearly and I would describe her as one half of my very nearly perfect parents, I will also go as far as to say she can be very challenging, stubborn, and difficult just for the sake of it! Common traits in most of us, I would suggest. So, as I have said before, not everything is about dementia.

However, occasionally she does acknowledge her memory issues, saying things like, "I can't remember what I had for breakfast, but I can remember my mum teaching me how to sweep the stairs and polish the brass bars." She may then add, "Isn't that strange?"

She usually finishes this kind of statement with something like, "But it's not a problem – I remember the important things and I don't do anyone any harm." She refuses to entertain any kind of deeper conversation or exploration related to questioning her health and wellbeing.

Mum's attitude towards and understanding of her situation is admirable, as is her firmness around being in control of any *next steps* in relation to her condition – or any other element of her life, for that matter. Her tenacity and drive for independence, and being her own person, is what has enabled her to lead such a full and interesting life – and she has no intention of giving any of that up just because she has a dodgy memory. She has had to lay down the law on this point on several occasions, particularly when we have tried to encourage her, with her best interests at heart, to have an assessment and possible diagnosis.

The last time this happened, she had been through a day of intense confusion – which, as you can imagine, really drains her energy as well as knocks her confidence. On this occasion the confusion was the culmination of a kind of domino effect triggered by a small incident earlier on in the day that she didn't seem to be able to move forward from. Thankfully, later that evening she became far more lucid and felt good, and it was at this point she, once again, mentioned her struggles with following what is happening. Seeing an opportunity, I gently suggested we could go to the doctors, and they may be able to find out more about what was going on and possibly give her some medication to help improve her short-term memory or at least prevent it getting worse. This conversation did not go well – she felt very strongly that I was trying to coerce her into doing something she did not want to do – and I suppose I was.

This event, just like the Cyprus incident, caused her to see me in a different light, and it was clear that, for a while, she did not trust me. I had always been her ally, and suddenly she felt like I had been having conversations about her and making plans behind her back. It was a sad time, and I felt like I'd undermined her and let her down. Of course, I can understand her resistance to having an appointment and an assessment that might lead to some kind of diagnosis that would come with an inevitable label. She doesn't like being labelled at the best of times, and whatever label they gave her wouldn't be a positive one. She doesn't want special treatment, and she certainly doesn't want any sympathy – she just wants to be left in peace to carry on being a wife, a mother, and a friend.

Of course, there are many reasons why it makes sense for her to have an assessment and a formal diagnosis. No diagnosis means no access to services, medication or treatments that could help as the illness progresses. But Mum has capacity and the right to make an informed decision, and the very nature of a memory assessment requires that the individual proactively participates.

This has been a very tough issue that regularly raises its head as we continue our journey together through my mum's dementia. I am hopeful that when the time is right, she will agree to have an assessment, but time will tell. According to research, more than a third of people with the disease in the UK go undiagnosed, and at this point my mum is one of them. But for us, for the time being, we just continue to live in the moment, taking one day at a time.

The Wildebeest

When I was growing up there was a woman in the village we referred to as the Wildebeest. This wasn't meant as an insult; it was just in reference to her constantly walking. We saw her all over the place. It was a kind of game – who can spot her first. She lived in a caravan on a small site next to the river in Roydon. I don't know what her name was or her story, and I'm not sure why she walked so much. Maybe she was unable to ride a bike, or perhaps she hadn't the money to use buses or trains. When I saw her walking, she always seemed to be deep in thought, as if she was trying to work something out. She was definitely walking with purpose to a destination, either physical or psychological. Looking back through my rose-tinted glasses, I like to imagine that she walked because it was good for her body, good for her soul and maybe she was figuring out the big questions in life. If that is the case, then now, all these years later, I get it, and I reach out to her across the years as a fellow wildebeest.

I think best when I am on the move, particularly under my own steam. To be honest, I find it hard to sit still for any length of time. I think this is something I have inherited from my mum; she is a woman who is always going somewhere – another wildebeest at heart.

If I am struggling with an issue or a situation, staying put without moving often takes me down an abandoned rabbit hole that can lead to the dreaded *what ifs*. When this happens, my chain of thought is at risk of spiralling out of control, resulting in an unhealthy mindset that disables my ability to be optimistic. I have found that the best way to avoid this spiral, and to redirect my thinking in a more positive direction, is to get up and move my body, and in doing so broaden my perspective and shift my mindset. Sometimes, it's a conscious decision – *I am going to move away from this spot and away from this thinking.* I am not only moving through the physical world, from one point towards another, but also through the psychological world from one way of thinking to another. It's a kind of internal and external exploration that usually results in a shift in perspective as well as place, and it enables me to see things from a different and often wider viewpoint.

As Mum's condition has advanced, we have noticed she is spending more and more time on the move. Going from one room to another, using her new hips to head up the stairs and then come down again, constantly wanting to go out for a walk or pop round the shop.

Sometimes, I hear people living with dementia being described as "wandering without purpose." I don't believe this is the case; I believe that all behaviour is communication, so if somebody is walking, even if they appear to have no purpose, they are looking for something either internal or external. It could be an object, a place, a feeling, an answer, or they could be looking for the familiar – a link. This is the case with my mum, and as I say it is something the two of us have in common.

* * *

Today is one of those days when I need to be on the move, and I am walking. It's late spring 2019. It's chilly, and a bit damp, but the morning sun is up there somewhere, trying to break through the grey blanket of low, misty cloud. As I leave home, I can hear the blackbird singing, a tiny sign to remind me that the world is still turning and will continue to do so. This little bird has been around for two or three years. I know this because its repeated little tune sounds uncannily like "Spinning Around" by Kylie Minogue. In the past Simon has said he can hear it too, but I get the feeling he's humouring me. I like to hear the little bird, whom I should really call Kylie despite it being very likely he's male. The only problem is that every time I hear him sing, I find "Spinning Around" on repeat in my head, and today is no different.

I'm already walking with some pace. I can feel my muscles working, and I'm breathing hard. It's a good feeling. But, although "Spinning Around" is a great pop song, I really need to put a different record on the jukebox. Not an easy thing to do when Kylie's influence has even reached across species.

My day started with me thinking about my parent's situation and the 120 miles between us. The distance makes things difficult, because any problems that arise in Essex have a kind of time lapse that prevents me from being able to help when it's most needed. To use a popular metaphor, it's like dropping a pebble in the water: It's a small splash in Clacton, but with the ripple effect it expands, and by the time it gets to Sussex has often become something far more significant and difficult to deal with. So, when I think about Mum and Dad's wellbeing, one of the main barriers is one of geography. This distance and time issue is exacerbated by the fact that my dad doesn't like to phone me if he is struggling, as he doesn't want to worry me. I understand and can relate to this; it's far easier to tell people that are important to you that things are going well as opposed to sharing challenges and difficulties.

I remember one time when I was on a cycling trip in Australia. Rather than it being the life-changing physical and spiritual experience I had hoped it would be, it was, instead, a journey through a dark cloud of personal mental un-health, the like of which I'd never known before. Despite feeling isolated and desperate on the other side of the world, I didn't feel that I could be honest with anyone about what was happening to me. Looking back, I think there were two main reasons for this:

1) I didn't want to admit to what I saw as failure – even to myself.
2) I didn't want to unload my struggles onto somebody else, especially the people I loved.

So, I chose to be dishonest. I wrote deceiving postcards and aerogrammes describing an amazing journey through rain forests, coral seas and deserts that had little similarity to the journey I was taking. The strange thing is that describing this alternative experience helped me keep some kind of control of my spiralling and chaotic feelings of low self-esteem. I don't know if this is a good thing or not, but stepping into this parallel universe that people had no reason to question provided some kind of pause and respite from reality.

To be honest, recently, I haven't been phoning home as often as I could or should do. I'm not sure of my reasons; maybe just like that time in Australia, I'm, once again, sticking my head in the sand and avoiding the reality of the situation. Just thinking about this makes me feel selfish. Anyway, I haven't spoken to Mum or Dad for over a week, so I don't know how things are going, and as a result I am reading all kinds of catastrophes into the silence. But today, rather than biting the bullet, jumping out of bed, and giving my parents a call or even driving up to visit, I stayed in bed thinking about what might be happening, what the future might look like, and feeling guilty as well as a bit useless. Eventually I got out of bed, ate some toast, drank some hot tea, put my trainers on and headed out into the fresh air, and here I am.

* * *

What started off as a relaxed walk has now turned into a hike, which has taken me up through the woods on the South Downs of England above where I live. Stopping to catch my breath, I turn to look back in the direction I came, and I struggle to identify our house amongst all the others. Every detail is so familiar to me, but looking from a different viewpoint, from high above, and at a distance, it's hard to spot it. Trying to piece together familiar components into something that makes sense to me so I can identify where I am in relation to my home is a little frustrating. I realise my mum must regularly have similar frustrating experiences to this, when the pieces don't quite fit together as they should do. Eventually I notice a point of reference and follow the roads and tracks to find my house. It's almost incomprehensible that all those other little buildings and rectangles of green contain other people with their lives, relationships, challenges and, hopefully, happiness. I guess we are all at the centre of our own universe, and everything and everyone else orbits around us. Only a few seconds of exploring this concept is overwhelming. My mind boggles, and I move on.

As I continue with pace, the trees look fantastic with new buds and dripping leaves projecting a fresh green haze over the woodland. The ground is damp and spongy with rotting logs, vegetation, mosses and ferns. Some of the trees are old, knotted and twisted with small hollows and caves, which, I notice, local children have put little front doors on for fairies and pixies to live in.

I remember coming up here with Mum and Dad, a couple of years ago. When she saw these little secret dwellings, complete with front doors and post boxes, Mum stepped into the imaginary world the kids had created and started talking about the little souls who lived behind each door. This was irresistible for me, so I joined her in her musings, and for a few minutes we stepped back into the world we inhabited together when I was a little boy sitting on the orange rug with Carny the farting Labrador, while Mum fed my imagination with magical stories of dormice and elves.

Now, in recognition of this memory, I stop to clear some leaves away from one of the front doors – just in case a tiny being is struggling behind it. I am, and always will be, my mother's son.

* * *

The path is steep, and my heart is working hard. The traffic noise from the dual carriageway I crossed, by way of a green zigzag footbridge, has died away and been replaced by birdsong and the breeze. I left home about thirty minutes ago, and I have continued contemplating the problem that had woke me this morning, but my thinking has already shifted from, *what if something terrible happens and I can't get to my parents' house on time*...to, *what if we lived closer to each other, how great would that be?*

As I climb higher, I am getting warm and start to sweat. In my head I make a list all the benefits of us living closer together. It would be the best solution to all kinds of issues that may arise. We could see each other every day. Simon and I could be on hand if there was a crisis, we could share responsibilities so my dad could have respite and not feel so isolated (he hasn't said this is how he feels, but I imagine, at times, he does), and we could get a better understanding of how things actually are, as opposed to us finding solace by way of my dad's filter of kindness. It just makes so much sense to reduce those 120 miles, but it still feels like an impossibility.

It would mean either me and Simon moving up to Essex and finding a place to live, as well as new jobs, or Simon staying in Sussex and me going alone and moving in with my parents. Both options would be very difficult to achieve and would put enormous stress on all concerned. The alternative would be that they relocate to be close to us, but there is no way they could cope with the upheaval. Financially it would be a struggle if not impossible and, in addition to this, Mum's set routine and familiar surroundings play a major role in enabling her to live well with her illness, so moving may have a detrimental effect and possibly enable her dementia to take the upper hand. I mull this over as I walk, and realise that I must accept that, on this point, there is no easy solution. Feeling a bit deflated about the situation, I continue my walk but make a deal with myself to, at least, phone Mum and Dad every other day from now on.

At the top of the hill, I stop and peer into the dew pond. I had never heard of dew ponds until I met Simon, and he explained that they are manmade and are usually found on top of hills, their purpose being to provide water for livestock while also benefiting wildlife. Despite what their name suggests, dew ponds' main source of water comes from rainfall. I'm not sure how common they are, but up here on the South Downs there are quite a few.

Looking east from where I stand, there are views across Shoreham and Brighton to the white chalk cliffs of the Seven Sisters. In the foreground is the River Adur with its strong tidal currents and mud flats, above which is perched the fabulously gothic, and ridiculously *Hogwarts-esque*, Chapel of Lancing College. Looking south, and out towards the English Channel, where the sky and the water meet, there are swathes of giant hovering wind turbines, behind which pass container ships from around the globe making silent progress towards their destinations.

Next to the dew pond is a bench that has been placed here as a memorial to a local man. Engraved across its length is his name, his dates of birth and death and the inscription:

"Please give up this seat for a young person."

I love this. In a world where young people get such a bad press and are judged and blamed for everything, it's refreshing to be reminded that they are the future, and they deserve to be valued and respected just as much as anybody else. The dates tell me that, sadly, this hero of equality and inclusion didn't live to an old age, but I get the feeling he made the most of the time he did have; I do hope so.

Taking a seat, I turn my attention back to the flatlands to find the tiny plot that Simon and I have made our home and wonder if somewhere down there is another plot that could do the same for my parents. The breeze gets up and goose-bumps around my neck tingle, reminding me that I am supposed to be walking, rather than sitting on this great man's bench. I decide I'd better get moving and focus on what is possible today, so I continue my journey and follow *The South Downs Way* heading west.

The sun has now broken through, and there are expanding areas of blue sky winning the battle for dominance over the clouds that are slowly diminishing. As well as taking some time out in nature to breathe fresh, clean air into my lungs, raise my heart rate and clear my thinking, my walk today has another purpose, and that is to visit Cissbury Ring. My route takes me over chalky hills, which are criss-crossed by giant waltzing pylons carrying power to secluded houses, farms, and villages. I also pass trenches dug to carry power from the offshore wind farm to a power plant on the north side of the Downs. I guess over time this new technology will lead to the demise of the prehistoric pylons and their fizzing cables.

An hour later and approaching my destination, I pass another well-used dew pond, this time encircled by a five-metre band of muddy hoof prints. Obviously, this is used by both wild and domestic animals. Above the middle of the pond, I notice an intense swirling column of hundreds, if not thousands, of tiny insects spiralling in a tall and silent tornado. Below them small birds are swooping down into the shallows, collecting mud as a building material for their nests; they are most likely house martins but I'm not completely sure.

According to the sign at its base, Cissbury Ring is the second largest hillfort in England. It has a long and varied history stretching back over five thousand years. During this time, it has been used as an ancient burial site, a Neolithic flint mine, and as a training ground for the Normandy landings in World War II. It is amazing to think that so much of human history could have taken place up on this hill – reading these few details subtly changes my view and relationship to the ground I am walking on. I am enjoying the idea of moving through the physical world, right now in the moment, while also tiptoeing back through time, imagining the people and their structures, as well as their hardships and achievements. They must have overcome unimaginable challenges just to survive. This thought serves to remind me what a gift it is to be living this life, on this planet with so much potential beyond what we see as possible.

The climb up to the top is steep and breathtaking. Once I reach level ground, I wander around imagining what life might have been like for the people who settled here over the centuries. It strikes me that, using my phone, I can access information about what took place on this spot in the distant past, but I have no way of knowing what took place here yesterday or this morning. Is this what it feels like for my mum? She can access distant memories, but the recent past is shrouded in mist.

As I take a break and survey the world below, I enjoy the feeling of achievement that comes with making it to the top of this pretty hard climb. On a clear day, which it now is, the view is spectacular. Today I can scan the coastline from Beachy Head in the east all the way to the Isle of Wight, which floats on a misty horizon in the southwest. Turning, and looking north across the Weald, I can see the North Downs in the far distance, and in the foreground the strangely slow and silent airplanes approaching Gatwick Airport.

* * *

I think back twelve years to the last time I visited this place. It was a completely different experience, which left me and my friends with a distinctly unsettled feeling in our bones. It was midwinter, on a day when the sun had so little strength that everything seemed to be in black, white, and chilly greys. Simon and I were walking with our dear friends, Nick and Mel. We also had a couple of dogs with us and a flask of home-made sloe gin, the purpose of which was to provide occasional sips to ward off the cold. When we arrived, it was far colder than expected, so we ditched the *little and often* plan and opted, instead, to neck the gin in a car park before setting off.

I think we must have come from the south because the climb was longer and the terrain more varied than the route I have taken today. As we climbed the steep and foggy track, we passed through what seemed like layers of different land-scapes. Open, chalky scrubland turned into areas dominated by shrubs and bushes, which in turn became thick wooded areas leading into rocky clumps and grassland. At one point we entered a closed-in holloway – an ancient, natural, sunken path – that wound its way around gnarly roots and boulders beneath a canopy of evergreen foliage, creating a green, damp, and subdued environment that felt like it had developed its own little ecosystem. The holloway deepened as the path dropped, to become a kind of ditch with plants clinging to its steep banks of soil, stone, moss, and ferns. Hidden in this secret passageway, there was a large entrance to some kind of burrow that we assumed must be a badger set. It looked aban-doned, no fresh tracks, just a cobweb strung across the open-ing, hoping to snare something in the space where light meets dark. Simon pointed out that an abandoned badger set would be "a great place to hide a dead body, as it is made by animals rather than humans and nobody would think of looking in it."

Leaving the holloway, we walked out into open grassland, lumpy with large rocks, and criss-crossed with paths created by generations of use by different creatures that had made this place their home. We headed towards a stand of trees that between them seemed to be holding onto a blanket of light, sepia-coloured mist. On entering we heard hushed voices, which for a second unnerved me. Then, coming into a small clearing, we met two men who were, thankfully, not enlarging a badger set but instead preparing to fly birds of prey that they had perched on their outstretched arms.

Nick, ever curious, and a naturally social animal, went to strike up a conversation to find out more. But these two chaps weren't up for a chat and said that our strange and unfamiliar voices would unsettle the birds. This made perfect sense, so taking the hint we walked away, but as we did so Nick, rising above this *brush-off*, called a hearty farewell to them, waved, and wished them a great day. They each made a grimace, ignored him, and turned their backs.

There was something of *The Deliverance* about this brief encounter, and I wouldn't have been wholly surprised to hear the "Dueling Banjos" being carried through the trees and across the grey landscape on the breeze. To lighten the slightly sinister mood these two guys had left with us, I referenced the film by telling Nick he had *mighty pretty lips* – which, of course, he does.

As we made our way along the edge of the ancient ditch that had been dug over three thousand years ago to circumnavigate the hill, we noticed one of the birds of prey was now flying silently and with purpose through the bare trees, weaving between hillocks and burial mounds, and then soaring high above to scan the ground for any movement. The soundless but powerful presence of the birds seemed to add to the otherworldliness of the place on this particularly dark and wintery day.

We stood at what we decided was the centre of the ring and wondered what the area must have looked like before the great storm of 1987, which had destroyed many of the trees. And, like today, looking back much further into history, we tried to imagine all the people who had visited or lived here over thousands of years. We all agreed that this place certainly felt like it had retained something of those long-forgotten lives. Then Simon, cashing in on the atmosphere of the place and the tone of our conversation, wondered, in all that time, how many people had been murdered up here. We all looked at him and remembered that he had been the main culprit in polishing off the sloe gin, and he was now giggling with a grave look on his face.

Suddenly, Dudley the black Jack Russell started barking and chasing something that wasn't there. "Right, that's it, I'm out of here!" declared Nick. And we made our way back down to the car park to look for a pub. Notwithstanding Simon's efforts to introduce a more ominous element to the day than was actually evident, I must say that the experience still left an impression, and since that time I have remembered Cissbury Ring as a beautiful but eerie place with a noticeably strange atmosphere about it. Not exactly threatening, but a little disconcerting. As a result of this, I have found myself compelled to revisit the site and get an update on my perceptions, so that is why I am here today.

* * *

I am standing at the top of the hill taking in the view, then, convincing myself an extra few feet will extend my field of vision, I decide to climb on top of the trigpoint.

Trigpoints are a nationwide network of small concrete pillars that are placed on high ground and are connected to their closest neighbours by a direct line of sight. Each one is topped by a three-armed brass plate known as a *spider,* which is used to cradle a contraption called a *theodolite*, the purpose of which is to measure relative positions, in order to map the exact shape of the land. Their connections form an invisible network, a few feet above the ground, that stretches from coast to coast, across the whole country.

Today I am standing on the concrete trigpoint, not using

it for science, but maybe for spirit.

This is not the place I remember. The sun is now shining, and the sky is blue. There are no shady characters, or sinister activities. No ghostly spectres, or dark places hiding bodies. But there are two wild birds of prey patrolling the skies. One large and riding on thermals in ever decreasing spirals, probably a buzzard, and one smaller, no doubt a kestrel, which is hovering above a ditch, its head perfectly still, and level with my eye line. I'm pleased to say that neither bird is tethered to a handler.

Wow! This is beautiful. If I had one, I could pitch a tent and sleep up here. My original take on this place has been shattered and replaced by something wild and spectacular, but I am happy to report that it hasn't lost its otherworldliness – there is still an air of magic about it. Once again, I am reminded of the value of looking through a different lens with an open mindset, and a willingness to take on board views that may challenge my previous viewpoints.

An hour later I am back at the bench by the dew pond, and as there is no younger person about, I take a seat and look down to find the house that feels so unique when I'm in it, but from here it is just one small block in a hotchpotch of terraced houses, flats, schools, and shops. My walk up to Cissbury Ring has helped me recalibrate how I am seeing the world, broadening my horizons both visually and psychologically.

As I make my way back down to sea level, I realise that following my little adventure, I'm now not seeing an impossible challenge; I'm seeing real possibility and potential. Maybe down there somewhere below me there is a plot that could become my parents' home. Maybe there is a way of affording it, and maybe the long-term benefits to all our wellbeing would outweigh any short-term problems. Seeing things in this way does not solve all the issues, but adopting this mindset does make things feel more achievable than they felt a couple of hours earlier. The idea of us living close together is now in a file boldly labelled: *Possibly, Maybe.*

The Golden Ticket

It's Christmas Day 2019. Eight months since my walk over the South Downs. As with most years, Mum and Dad are staying with us for the festive season. Simon, being a great cook, has produced an amazing Christmas dinner with all the trimmings, and now we are pulling crackers, and, much to my dad's dismay, putting on our paper party hats. Any sniff of *dressing up*, and he usually threatens to leave the country and retract any festive goodwill comments he may have uttered. But surprisingly, on this occasion, he agrees to put on the hat with minimal protest, provided no photographs will be taken. This last point is a red flag to Simon, who immediately starts taking stealth snaps while we all chatter.

The jazz classic, *A Charlie Brown Christmas* by The Vince Guaraldi Trio, is playing on the sound system. For me at least, there is no better soundtrack to evoke the magic of being a little kid at Christmas, but like the cartoon, this music is relevant to all ages, and the jazz element triggers a story from my dad that we haven't heard before.

He is telling us that, as teenagers, he and his best mate John would put on their coolest outfits and drive in Dad's Hilman Minx to a car park in a little town called Hoddesdon, where they would put John's record player on the bonnet of the car and play jazz records to attract potential girlfriends. In preparation, they had even been to dancing lessons so were fully equipped to impress with moves and shapes, if the need arose. I'm not sure if the dance had a name but it must have been quite formal because it included the occasional salute to the young ladies they were attempting to woo.

As I write this, I realise that this ambitious and go-getting duo may well have been the original boy-racers with their booming bass, eye-catching outfits and snazzy moves. We are all laughing as he tells this tale. Then Mum, totally connecting with his story, tells us that was how she met him – the love of her life – dancing with his mate in a car park in Hoddesdon. As she picks up where he left off, she adds so many extra details that it simply must be true... And it becomes a new truth for all of us.

Simon, being an audiophile, is fascinated by the record player – how was it powered? Was it wind-up? If so, did you have to stop mid-dance to rewind it? Visions of the two lads having to start off quickly and then slow the pace along with the record as it ran out of steam are explored with much laughter. To bring the experience to life, Simon is using the internet to find and play Dad and John's favourite tracks of the time – but we cannot tempt a dance demonstration.

Then suddenly, "Excuse me, excuse me!" Mum interrupts and changes the subject with a volume, tone and confidence that leaves us little choice but to stop talking and turn our attention to her. As seems to have become a tradition, she is collecting up the cracker jokes and announces she is going to read them out. It's so good that she feels confident enough in the present company to do this.

She was not in a good place early this morning. One minute she was lucid and comparatively sure of herself, but then in no time at all her memory issues really seemed to kick in, she became overwhelmed, and it was clear that she was desperately trying to get a grip on what was happening. This experiential roller coaster, now a regular occurrence, translated into emotional turmoil, for her and for us, the people who love her. I can't imagine what this kind of event is like for my dad when they are at home in Essex by themselves. This morning's episode is understandable. She woke up in an unfamiliar room, she didn't know where she was or why she was there, she had even forgotten it was Christmas. So, if you think about it, it doesn't take a great deal of effort to imagine how that would make you feel.

It is at these times of increased confusion that it's even more important for us to be vigilant, respectful, and subtle in supporting her to gain some level of understanding and control of her situation. Today this was comparatively easy to achieve. Being Christmas Day, there were clues everywhere: decorations, tinsel, cards, and the smell of food being prepared. So, although she arrived downstairs with a look of worry and uncertainty on her face, we were soon able to reassure her and remind her what was happening and that she was in the right place with the right people – where she belongs.

The cracker jokes are predictably terrible – that's their role – people expect mediocracy not wit, and today they have delivered the goods. But this is about much more than the comedy of bad jokes; it's about strengths, and one of the many skills that has been maintained, despite an illness – the ability to read. Some of the jokes are so bad we are left bewildered, but the reader has managed to use them to put herself back in the centre of the conversation with all our attention and laughter.

* * *

My next-door neighbours are away in Scotland, and I have a key to their house. I tell Mum I'm popping next door, as they have asked me to keep an eye on the heating, and I ask does she want to come and have a look? Being a curious woman, she jumps at the chance to check it out. In the event, all four of us have trudged next door and are standing in the lounge looking down the garden. Mum loves it.

"Imagine living here, Guy; all this space and a lovely big garden."

Simon chips in, "And you would be living next door to us." At hearing this, Mum makes a quip about there being a downside to everything.

"Would you really like to live here?" asks Dad.

"I'd love it," she replies.

"But wouldn't it be sad to leave our house in Clacton?" A good question, as one of her repeated narratives is all about how much she loves living where they do and that she would never want to move.

"I would be sad, but it would be lovely living here, with all this space, those curtains, that carpet and the boys next door."

"Well, I'm pleased about that because I've bought it for you – Happy Christmas!"

She is astounded and thinks he's joking, so it takes a few minutes to convince her that this is fact, and the house will soon belong to the two of them. The penny drops. Suddenly we are in an emotional, tearful, excited, and shocked whirlwind of questions, hugs, and kisses. I am surprised by how emotive it is, we all have tears in our eyes. My mum is over the moon, and my dad is relieved he can now share what is happening. Eventually we head back next door.

Mum has kept the emotional residue of what has happened – a kind of euphoria – but she has soon forgotten the reason for these feelings. We spend a lot of time over the next few days reminding her about the move, and then trying to convince her it's true.

This is a momentous occasion. My dad has dreamed of living in that house for a long time. It has everything he would like, including a very nice garage and workshop, which he has been coveting since he first saw it (that workshop was my dad's *Chanel handbag*). However, this was never going to happen; it would be too expensive, too big an upheaval for my mum, and fraught with risk on many levels.

Then, suddenly, our neighbours decided to put their house on the market and move. Although I knew it was an impossibility, I decided to call my dad to at least explore if there was any way we could make it happen – after all, we both knew very well that Mum's condition was advancing, meaning she needed more support, and things were probably going to continue heading in that direction. We also knew that it was highly likely that at some point things would need to change and my parents would need a wider support network. But on top of this, as well as family, we are all great friends, enjoying each other's company whenever we are together. Maybe I really did need to explore the possibility of moving to Essex, or we could get carers to come to the house and give my mum some support and my dad some respite. That could work, but my mum's headstrong, and dare I say stubborn, streak would not make this an easy option. Or – and this was the golden ticket – maybe something would happen that would enable them to move down to be closer to Simon and me, and then we could live happily ever after.

Well, something did happen. Dad and I had a very open and honest conversation, recognising that this was a one-off and life-enhancing opportunity that should not be missed if possible. We both agreed to think it through overnight and come back to the table in the morning. To be honest, I really didn't think it would happen – there were as many reasons not to move as there were reasons to move. However, the long-term benefits could not be underestimated.

That evening, Simon and I also had an open and honest conversation. He was wonderful:

"Of course they should move, they'd be mad not to!" We discussed the potential barriers, the obvious one being money. Simon suggested we extend our mortgage to make up the shortfall my dad may have. I couldn't believe he suggested this – I am a lucky man to have him in my life.

The next day my dad phoned me early in the morning. I was shocked and elated that he had decided to go for it and pull out all the stops to make this move happen. It turned out that they could manage the move... There really was a golden ticket!

We knew that, overall, Mum would be in favour of the idea. She often spoke about living closer to us, and how lovely that would be. She is a social person and, if she is feeling confident, being with the people she loves will always come out tops. On several occasions, she had also mentioned to me her concerns that if anything should happen to her or my dad, it would be a good idea for us to be on hand. This wasn't a request; it was just an observation. In truth, I had been having similar thoughts.

Due to her tending to get very anxious about new plans that aren't definite and predictable, my dad decided not to tell his wife about the new house until it was in the bag and even the moving date was arranged. Hence this lovely situation we find ourselves in on Christmas Day.

Clint Eastwood and the Three Conspiracies

May 2020. "What do you think of Covid-19? I think it's all made up and doesn't really exist – it's just not true," says the young, handsome removals man with an Eastern European accent.

Then he continues by asking, "Do you know anybody with it, with the virus I mean?" I shake my head.

"Nobody does," he says. "It only happens to people we don't know; it's a giant lie."

I consider challenging his thinking. After all, the company he works for has delayed our moving date by four months due to Covid-19 restrictions and lockdowns, etc., and we are speaking through masks, so there must be something to it. However, my focus today is for the contents of Mum and Dad's house in Essex to be relocated to their new home in Sussex, with no hassle and as little damage as possible. So, entering any kind of disagreement about worldwide conspiracy theories would not be useful at this point, and it certainly wouldn't get us to our destination any quicker.

The move started a few weeks ago when the tropical fish tank and its residents headed south and set up home in the house next door to ours. Then the following weekend I hired a van, drove up to Clacton and loaded up the entire contents of the tool shed and greenhouse, plus all my dad's favourite plants, and a few he felt sorry for. Then I hit the road and took them all to join the fish in Sussex.

There were more journeys back and forth moving about thirty years of accumulated paraphernalia down south. While this was happening, my brother Martin and his partner Helen helped clear a lot of possessions that weren't going to move, and they also gave the house a deep clean. But as it turns out, this *phased* approach to moving, although useful, gave us a false sense of security about how hassle-free the actual moving day would be. But now that day has arrived, Dad and I realise that this assumption was a little naive. The facts are we have shed loads to do, we have hired a dodgy removals company who don't seem to be very clued up on the art of packing a lorry and, in addition to this, their experience of actually having done any removals is becoming questionable. There seems to be a never-ending procession of furniture, crates, and mystery packages leaving the house and although the lorry is looking full up, the house doesn't seem to be any emptier.

* * *

While we are spending the day stressing about the move, Simon and Mum have set off early in the car heading south with Ronnie the Jack Russell, Milo the pug, and some other essential bits and pieces. We definitely drew the short straw, but the main thing here is ensuring this major upheaval has a minimum negative impact on Mum as possible.

As I empty the TARDIS-like cupboard under the stairs, I wonder what they are talking about and imagine myself sitting in the back seat of the car listening in to their private conversation. Mum will be in charge of subject matter, and I'm pretty sure she will be telling Simon some of her favourite stories. Maybe she's talking about the beginnings of the NHS and the handsome doctors she flirted with as a young woman. Picking up on this, Simon will ask if she went out on dates with any of them, which she didn't, but ignoring this he will push for potentially sordid, and even sexy, details. There won't be any (as far as I know...), but this will make her laugh – she loves her little private chats with him. In some ways I think she opens up to him in ways that she wouldn't with me.

As they are travelling in the car, she may well be telling him about when she passed her driving test first time despite nobody believing she was capable. This is a great story that she tells with real relish in her voice, enjoying this one of many examples of when she has triumphed in the face of adversity. As they cross the Queen Elizabeth 2 (QE2) Bridge, looking towards the skyline of the city of London, she could be sharing her memory of witnessing the red and orange glow on the horizon as London burnt during the Blitz in 1940. This will lead onto stories of air raid shelters, gas masks or maybe the two significant bombs. But perhaps, seeing the silhouette of the city, she will instead be speaking about when, as teenagers, she and her friend Rosemary would head up to Highbury to watch Arsenal play.

Although familiar with these stories, Simon will be coming from a place of hearing them for the first time, and he will undoubtedly be asking questions and encouraging her to elaborate, enabling her to add often funny, new details, and in doing so grow more confident and prouder of her extraordinary life.

Whatever the subject of the conversation, I am pretty sure that any moments of silence will result in her asking why Simon is driving, where are they going, and where is Guy. This will probably be repeated throughout the journey as, although she likes being a passenger in the car and she really enjoys the drive, she is used to my dad being by her side – they very rarely go anywhere without each other – so seeking clarity would be the natural thing to do.

I wonder if she is talking about the move. After all, today is a very significant and life-changing day for all of us. It may well have slipped her mind, but that doesn't matter. I am pretty sure that she is having a lovely time and finding comfort in sharing whatever is on her mind right now in the moment with her "third (and possibly favourite!) son."

* * *

Meanwhile, Dad and I are soldiering on trying to get to grips with what needs doing and what needs to be where. The two young removals men look hungry and skinny; they also have an air of desperation about them, as if they are trying to make ends meet in a world that is seemingly against them. This has led me to develop my own conspiracy theory, the second of the day, and I am now convinced that they are being exploited by their employers and are not being paid properly – if at all. As we all busy ourselves packing furniture and loading the lorry, my theory has grown legs, and by the time we stop for a coffee break I have them down as full-blown victims of modern-day slavery, living in a cold, cramped caravan or lorry container on an industrial estate somewhere in the East End of London. Considering this, I ply them with Kit Kats and crisps, half convincing myself that this will make everything OK and improve the unfortunate situation they have, no doubt, found themselves in. My theory casts a slight shadow over my thinking. What on earth do these two young men make of us and our *stressful* situation of privilege? As this thought crosses my mind, I have a feeling of guilt and mild embarrassment, so I reach out to offer another Kit Kat.

Chocolate eaten, mugs emptied, and thoughts of modern-day slavery put to one side for the time being, we are all back focused on the task in hand. Dad and I are packing plates and pans in the kitchen, and our two colleagues are upstairs dragging furniture about. A while later one of them calls to us. He is coming down the stairs on the front end of a very rickety-looking wardrobe. In broken English he is telling us that this piece of furniture isn't in the best condition and he's not sure it will survive the journey. He tentatively goes on to suggest that maybe we should leave it behind, but before we have time to ponder his suggestion there is a sudden groan, a creaking noise, and a gasp. I'm not sure which noise came from the wardrobe, and which came from the second removals man who is hidden somewhere on the other end of it. The creak turns into a crash as the whole thing falls apart in painfully slow motion, leaving our two helpers holding onto a disintegrated wardrobe, and probably feeling slightly paranoid about how we will react.

A moment's silence while the dust settles, then Dad says, "Decision made, let's leave it here!"

Once the lorry has left and we have given the guys some money for McDonald's, we continue to clean up and pack boxes that need to be taken with us to the new house. It's not until we are alone that we have a chance to really acknowledge the scale of what is happening today. This is a monumental occasion. After thirty years of living in this house together, my parents are moving into a new home, in another part of the country, farther away from some family and friends, but crucially, next door to me and Simon.

The move is risky, scary, challenging, and absolutely the right thing to do. My dad is brave taking on such as significant change of life at his age, and in his situation. But this was a one-off opportunity that could not be missed, and if it all works out as we hope, the benefits and positive effect will far outweigh any adverse consequences – or that's what we keep telling ourselves. But it has been a rocky road just getting to this point, and as we chat, I start to realise the toll that this massive undertaking has had on my dad and his wellbeing. It sounds like the last six months have been very difficult, and at times it has been hard for him to lift his head up out of the maelstrom and focus on what he is trying to achieve and why. To put it simply, while all this legal, practical and above all complicated activity has been going on, it has been a challenge for him to keep his eye on the prize.

I go into the kitchen to make tea and, discovering the kettle is on its way south, I use an old saucepan to boil the water. I reflect on what he has been telling me. I can't begin to imagine what it's been like. He has been juggling finances, sorting through a lifetime of belongings, and identifying what needs keeping and what should go to the charity shop (not an easy task for a natural hoarder). On top of this he has been organising utilities, both for the house he is leaving and the one he is heading for, booking the removals men, and dealing with the endless list of practicalities that come with moving home.

Meanwhile Mum has spent much of this time with little or no awareness of the upcoming move; her short-term memory loss has seen to that, but when it has come up in the conversation she has been excited about the big things, particularly being close to Simon and me, and having a new house to live in. She also loves the idea that they are actually *doing this*. However, like with any major change, this move also comes with worries and recurring questions that need to be answered in a positive and empowering way. My dad takes this responsibility very seriously, but I know it has been tough for him, particularly when he is dealing with everything else, including lockdowns and pandemic restrictions. He feels that he has literally been thinking and planning for two – which of course he has.

Throughout this time, I have tried to be supportive, but from a distance. Now we are really talking about it, I realise that the distance was not only one of geography but also of time. I have had the luxury of stepping in and out of this situation while my dad has had to deal with it twenty-four hours a day for months on end.

I rejoin him sitting on garden chairs in the lounge. I ask more questions and hopefully provide him with the time and space to recount what his life has been like, and for me to acknowledge what an incredible achievement that is, and how thankful I am for him sticking with it for the greater good. I must point out that as he speaks about this, he isn't coming from a place of complaint or of being a victim – he is just talking about his experience and his relief that there is, at last, light at the end of the tunnel. We finish our tea with a grimace, the saucepan having infused it with more than a hint of old potatoes, then we get back to work loading the car and doing some last-minute cleaning.

Thinking about our conversation, it occurs to me that since my mum started to struggle with her dementia, which was a number of years ago, most of my conversations with my dad have been about his wife's health and happiness and what he is doing to maintain it. I have hardly ever really asked how he is doing. I feel a bit sick; why has this not occurred to me before? I have just assumed he is fine because he's my dad and his job is to be resilient and cope with whatever life throws at him – like he always has done. But the reality is that despite all of this, he is a human being and needs support and friendship as much as the next person. It would be impossible for anyone to step into his shoes and not be affected by the pressure he finds himself dealing with daily. Considering this, I decide that although I can't change what's gone before, I can resolve to be there for him and with him, from this moment onwards. I have always been immensely proud of my dad, but this whole house move business on top of my mum's dementia is on another level and is a fantastic example of why I will always continue to be so.

With the car now full of random *must keep* objects, we are heading south ourselves. We have the sun in our eyes so stop at a service station for takeaway coffee and for my dad to see if he can get some sunglasses. Once I'm back in the car with our drinks, I watch him strolling across the forecourt already wearing his cool, new Clint Eastwood-style shades. He really looks like Clint; he even has that same exasperated and suspicious *Grand Torino* swagger about him that Clint does so well.

I think to myself, *There's an old geezer with some attitude; I wouldn't want to get on the wrong side of him.* I tell him this when he gets in the car – he appreciates my observations and confirms that this was the look he was going for.

By the time we are crossing the QE2 bridge, my dad, being the king of suspicion, has developed his own conspiracy theory – the third of the day. He has convinced himself, and almost convinced me, that the entire contents of his house are now being sold off the back of a lorry at Brentwood Market, North London. This has practically been confirmed by Simon, who phoned to say he and Mum have been home for ages, but the furniture hasn't arrived yet, despite our friendly removals men having had plenty of time to get there.

My dad combines his theory with mine and says, "Well, if you were a modern-day slave, living in a tin box on an industrial estate while being ripped off by your employer, wouldn't you look for ways to make a quick bundle and do a runner?" He has a point.

So, on this action-packed day when, to be honest we have better things to do, we have all developed theories and our own version of the truth. Our wardrobe wrecker has decided that Covid-19 does not exist and is just made up by people who want to sell face masks. I am pretty sure that he and his mate are the victims of financial abuse and are earning money for some fat cat who doesn't give a damn about them, and my dad, a man of many theories, is convinced that his furniture has got a good price and is now being installed in houses across North London.

An hour later, we arrive home and are shocked to discover the removals men still haven't shown up.

Oh my god, he was right!

They are not here, and we certainly haven't passed them on the way down – so where are they? As we share the Brentwood Market theory with Mum and Simon, I seriously start to consider that maybe we have lost a lorry load of Mum and Dad's property. This is a nightmare; I am knackered, and the furniture has been stolen.

As I contemplate this, my shoulders drop, I lean on the wall and my world seems to slowly get dark.

Why us? Why today?

Then I turn around to face the window and realise why my world has gone dark: A tatty white lorry has pulled up outside and is blocking out the daylight. The removals men have arrived safely along with the unharmed and unsold furniture.

Before they leave, my dad gives them a healthy tip and wishes them well. As they drive away, he turns to me and says, "As soon as I met those two fellas, I knew we could trust them."

Clues and Trails

Today my dad has taken the car to the garage; I am sitting in my parents' lounge, hoping to keep Mum company. I can hear her upstairs getting dressed, moving things around, opening and closing cupboards, and generally pottering about.

I'm so pleased and relieved that they have moved into the house next door – what are the chances of that happening? I can't help thinking it was fate. I know it was a huge upheaval, particularly for my dad, and surprisingly less so for my mum. But now they have been living here for a couple of weeks, they are beginning to settle in, and we are already reaping the benefits of being neighbours.

My dad is adjusting to having some support and respite, as well as having a new house and garden to think about. Mum is enjoying having more people around her to spend time with and satiate her boundless need of social interaction, and Simon and I are adjusting to having them living next door, close enough to feel the benefits and far enough away that we all have the space to live the life we want to live. It's amazing how quickly this has all become the norm. I thought there would be a kind of transition, but we all just got on with it, and now it feels like we have been neighbours for years.

I hear her come carefully down the stairs, so I stand to put the kettle on. She is quietly talking to herself as she descends. I wonder what she is saying. I think I can make out counting; maybe she's counting the stairs. It goes quiet; the stairs aren't creaking, but it doesn't sound like she has reached the bottom. Then, movement and the low talking resumes; I realise she has turned around and is heading back up. She has either forgotten something or is a little confused and is looking for clues and information.

* * *

For over thirty years, every morning Mum has descended a staircase while holding onto a handrail on the left-hand side. On the wall above the rail hung familiar framed photographs of family events, friends and loved ones, pets, and places. Halfway down the stairs there was a landing with a small table. On the table sat a ceramic deer, which my parents were given on their wedding day, over sixty years ago. Like the photographs, this little deer was, and still is, a cherished and significant object. From the landing, the stairs changed direction and led down to a small hall.

Once in the hall, the kitchen was on the left, the lounge on the right, and the front door was straight ahead. The layout never changed and neither did the tall, wooden French dresser that stood to the left of the front door. The dresser had a waist-level shelf, and this is where keys, dog leads, pale pink lipstick, a hairbrush, and general odds and ends were deposited or collected depending on which direction you were heading, and what you were wanting to do. Below the shelf were two drawers. These were the kind of drawers that every house has at least one of. Their purpose was to accommodate homeless and often useless items that had not been thrown away as they may come in handy at some point, and the surprising thing is they often did. The contents of these drawers included small toys and trinkets from Christmas crackers, those things that help you thread a needle, blunt pencils, and plumbing tape. Although the drawers and the purpose they served were rarely valued, they were a good first port of call to look for random lost items that may have been stashed away if there was no other obvious place to put them. To the left of the dresser, attached to the wall, was a full-length mirror.

As Mum's dementia progressed, her journey down these stairs took on an extra significance and purpose. The familiar and emotive pictures and objects provided a kind of trail of clues and prompts that jogged her memory if needed, reminding her where she was and what was important. Once she was off the bottom step, she would check her appearance in the mirror. Most likely, she would then use the hairbrush and lipstick from the dresser to add final touches. She had probably already gone through this familiar ritual several times in front of the bathroom mirror upstairs, but she may not remember, and anyway it's always worth checking again. Once this was all done and she was ready to face the day, she would make her way into the kitchen to see who was there and seek out the next set of clues and important information.

Today, however, there is no familiar trail, and she has found herself in a significantly different environment. She is descending a straight staircase, which is steeper than the one she is used to. There is a handrail but it's on the right side rather than the left. This feels strange and a little bit back to front, so she is being extra vigilant. There is no midway landing or change of direction, and no wedding presents or photographs. At the bottom of the stairs, she is confronted by my dad's tropical fish tank. There is no French dresser, but there are some mystery doors leading to – who knows where? There is a mirror but no brush or pale pink lipstick. Is she in the right place?

Maybe that's why she has headed back upstairs. I'm thinking she is looking for the familiar. I attempt to remedy this by calling upstairs, "Morning Mum, it's Marcus. Dad has popped to the garage, so you are going to have to put up with your favourite son for a few hours; do you fancy a cup of tea on this sunny Monday morning?"

She calls back, "Morning, darlin', yes please!"

I have given her all the information she needs at this point, and she is soon heading back down the stairs again. She is speaking to Ronnie the Jack Russell who has also heard her coming and has excitedly made his way to the bottom of the stairs. He knows wherever his mum is there will always be a treat for him, and she knows that if Ronnie is present, she must be in the right place. Renee and Ronnie are good and dependable partners to each other.

She walks into the kitchen looking confident, and I tell her she looks healthy and beautiful, which she does – let's face it, we all need to hear that occasionally. I'm sure she will have some questions shortly, probably about any plans we have today – she will be hoping I say, "No plans, we are just going to stay here."

However, before that she asks, "Where's Guy?" And I remind her that he has popped to the garage.

* * *

Since moving house, Mum's experience of dementia has become noticeably more erratic and inconsistent on a day-to-day, or even hour-to-hour basis. At times she can really struggle with making sense of what is going on around her and why she is in this strange setting. She is adjusting to her new home and loves it, but there is still a lot to get used to and I can tell that, at this point, she often feels a little unsure and potentially vulnerable.

Like most people, when she is feeling this way, she really wants clarity, and if she can't find the reassurance she is looking for, she will try to remove herself and escape to normality by saying things like, "Let's go home, Guy." When she says *home,* she is of course talking about their house of thirty years – familiar and predictable with a sense of belonging. Then my dad gently reminds her that they *are* at home and this beautiful house belongs to the two of them. This information, and the sensitive approach he takes to providing it, usually gives her all she needs to step into the here and now and become confident and at ease with her new and exciting life. My dad is her rock, and she knows if he says everything is OK, then it is.

At other times she is more lucid and aware of where she is and what is happening. When this is the case, she is clearly happy with her new situation, and her humour, her stories, and her infectious drive to have fun raise the spirits of anyone who is lucky enough to be in the vicinity. This doesn't mean that her condition isn't present, it just means that she is in a place that enables her to take control and enjoy herself. These times are priceless and make everything worthwhile.

We knew when we planned the move that there would likely be some negative consequences for her in relation to her illness, and we were right in our thinking. But having weighed up the risks along with the obvious long-term benefits, we decided it was absolutely the right thing to do, and now we need to do all we can to ensure the transition is as smooth and positive as possible. This involves thinking about the physical, and human environment, and trying to see things from her perspective, which isn't as difficult as it sounds. We all have very similar needs in relation to information and routines that help us navigate our way through our day-to-day lives. The difference is that, for people with dementia, it isn't so easy to access that information or to retain it for any great length of time, so it needs to be available, accessible, and obvious at all times.

* * *

Now the removal boxes are mostly unpacked, and things are slowly settling down, it is time to think about turning this house into a home that works for my mum (and my dad, of course). To do this, we have to collaborate with, and learn from, the woman herself. After all, she is the expert in what she needs and, over the years, she has developed very effective strategies of her own. You see, like many people living with dementia, my mum is almost constantly on the look-out for clues. Clues to remind her where she is, why she is here, who she is with and what is going to happen next. These clues come in all kinds of guises, which we all use either consciously – for example, checking the clock to see what time it is, or unconsciously – for example, the smell of food cooking may give us an indication of how close we are to mealtimes or even what day it is.

Another vital source of easy-access information is people. If you need to know something, just ask and, if people are worth their salt, they will tell you what you need to know, however many times you repeat the question. So, it is essential that it is *safe* to ask questions without being exposed, patronised, or made to feel like a nuisance for asking again.

* * *

We have bought a showcase (I think that's what they're called). It's glass-fronted has glass shelves, a mirrored back, and an internal light. It is a beautiful thing, and Mum is over the moon with it. We are all sitting in the lounge with two boxes open in front of us. The first is full of mostly wrapped and packed ornaments, and it is this that we are going to unpack today. As I unwrap each item and pass it to her, if she can remember, she tells us its story. There are wedding presents, things bought from charity shops on the many excursions to Frinton with Jean from next door, and a family of little wooden animals bought at a zoo. There is also a glass paperweight with a picture of St Paul's Cathedral inside that had sat on Flo's bedside cabinet for as long as anyone can remember and, my favourite, a ceramic squirrel with a broken ear, which was bought because Mum felt sorry for it and thought it might get lonely.

Many of the items spark fresh memories, which she shares with us, but as she gently places each piece in the cabinet, her narrative changes, and other items are moved and shifted as she explains their relationship to each other and her reasons for positioning them as she does. These reasons are very much in the present – groups of animals, people and objects that would normally be grouped together, for example, a family of rabbits or a Nativity set with all key players present, are instead separated, and put into new groups. She knows they belong together, however, in the context of the task at hand – that being a multi-shelved display case and a lifetime collection of ornaments – she ignores the obvious connections and instead combines them into a community of interlinking relationships and responsibilities.

The family of giraffes look down on the Holy Mother and her baby, as being so tall they are often left out of things, and they can keep an eye out for King Herod and his soldiers who would harm the baby. Meanwhile, Joseph is standing next to a giant pair of Jack Russell condiments, and all three are smiling at each other while also enjoying the company of a mother duck and her ducklings. On another shelf, three wise men are being guided to the holy baby by three glass flamingos. This scene is overlooked by a large wooden robin and a blue tit, neither of which have ever seen a flamingo before. As Mum places each precious object on a shelf, she works out exactly where it should go and tells us the reason and the connection. At times – mid-placement – another scene on a different shelf catches her eye, resulting in a ceramic poodle and her pups being transferred from their role escorting the three kings on their journey east, to keeping an elderly lady company as she sat in her chair darning her husband's socks.

This is a wonderful and mesmerising experience. We each go with Mum on this journey of creative thinking, feeding back how nice her display looks and joking that she will keep coming back to move bits and pieces.

"Absolutely," she says. "Somebody will have to walk all of these dogs, and these little ducks will need a pond!"

The showcase has turned into a treasure chest of memories, stories, and creativity. It's like a biography that has been put together by my mum, with all of us as witnesses. This means we will be able to use it as a place of connection with history and memories, and hopefully, as a portal to affirmation and pride for my mum.

* * *

One week later and here we are with the second, much bigger, removals box. This time my dad is armed with picture hooks and a hammer. We are hanging pictures, standing framed photographs, and positioning larger ornaments around the house, again under Mum's direction. Now there is a trail of links and reminders on the wall as she comes down the stairs and along the hall. There are key items and pictures in each room, and her clock, whiteboard, and calendar, which, together, became her *go-to* place for clarity in their previous house, has now been established on the wall opposite her favourite chair in the lounge.

The position of her chair provides a clear line of sight, not only to information that is important to her, but also who is coming and going, and what's happening with the birds and squirrels in the garden. This last point also includes the still-surprising appearance of Simon or me coming to visit as we have now put in a gate between the two gardens so it's quite normal for either one of us to appear between the roses (or maybe I should say thorns!).

The work we have all put in over the past week has really helped establish this house as the place where my mum belongs, her home, and these random pictures and treasures serve not only as a trail of reminders and reassurance, but also as objects of reference to trigger or redirect conversations and lift the mood if needed.

I think about my habit of getting lost in Clacton when I go for a bike ride, and the frustration of not having a memorable and logical trail of clues to help me on my way. In my parents' new house, together we have created this trail, and my mum can now feel more confident in where she is heading and why. This can only be a good thing.

A Murder on the Beach

It's a sunny July morning – I've popped round to see our new neighbours to find out what needs doing as they adjust to their new life. Dad is still sorting things out following the move; he is itching to get into his workshop at the end of the garden to make it his own by finding a home for all his tools, gardening equipment and general bits and pieces. One of the many benefits of living next door to each other is that we can do things on the spur of the moment, and realising that now is the perfect time for him to get into his workshop and start moving stuff about, I suggest that Mum and I go out for a coffee. She is keen on this idea and immediately makes it her own by saying to my dad, "I'll take Marcus for a coffee, and you can get on with what you want to do without me getting under your feet."

I love the way she subtly reframes the plan. My dad gets some time to himself, I get treated to a coffee and cake, and my mum is clearly in charge, and has reaffirmed herself as the family carer and provider. Everyone is a winner. I learn so much from really paying attention to what she says and how she behaves. It's this that tells us how she wants to live her life.

Having parked the car on the seafront, we set off walking along the coastal path. We are still in the middle of the pandemic, and although the restrictions have been relaxed a little, we still have to wear masks inside and avoid other people. Both issues are a struggle for Mum to understand as she takes it all so personally. "But why do they want me to wear a mask?" And "Why do they want me to stay away from them?"

Being a very spontaneous social person, and a great lover of children, it's not long before she makes a sudden beeline for a young family with an infant and a baby. Social distancing has gone out of the window, her mask is down around her neck, and she is fussing around them and their children. It's at times like this when she is so in the moment and full of joy that I feel like the *No Fun Police* as I try, but fail, to get her to abide by the rules. Fortunately, this wonderful family immediately understand the situation and are very friendly and welcoming. Of course, where there are affable young families with cute children involved, I have no chance of tempting her to move on until she is ready.

Eventually, as we head away, she turns to them, points at me, and says, "This is my baby, be warned; eventually they grow up and start telling you what to do!" They laugh.

She is in her element, breaking the rules and making people laugh while she's at it. I hope our new acquaintances enjoyed that little interaction as much as she did. I need to relax and remember what Simon pointed out, that *people are kind* – these two were as keen to show off their cute kids as my mum was to make a fuss of them.

The path now meanders its way through tamarisk and holly bushes and eventually opens to a layered vista of a stony beach, a hazy low tide, and a blue horizon where the sea and sky merge into one. On the distant tideline we can see gulls and waders carefully stepping amongst rock pools looking for some easy pickings. Meanwhile, further along the beach, a lone crow is flying into the air and dropping shellfish onto the stones in the hope of smashing their shells and grabbing a well-earned meal.

As we stand and watch this activity, my mum is giving a running commentary. She is totally present and confident to describe what she is seeing. I tell her the names of some of the plants and birds – she thinks I'm making them up, and she may be right. Then she tells me about using a fishing net to catch sticklebacks with her friend Ken when they were youngsters. I ask what they did with the little fish they caught. "Named them and then put them back in the river of course!" she says with a smile.

"Of course!" I repeat, returning the smile. "That's exactly what I would do as well."

A line of three cormorants are flying low over the sea heading west. At first, I say they are shags, which causes a giggle and casts even more doubt over my knowledge of flora and fauna. Close by, Mum points out a little brown bird as it hops about between drops of water that sit like glass beads on the giant green and purple leaves of a sea kale. I spot a horned poppy waving its yellow head in the breeze while its silver foliage contrasts with a smooth red tablet that was once a common house brick, but on its journey along the coast has changed its identity to become a thing of beauty.

We stand together, mesmerised by the scene around us, occasionally pointing things out to each other. I love this – there is no illness here, no need for short-term memory, no threats, no worries; just us, the space we occupy in the natural world around us.

A dog barks somewhere behind us and breaks the spell.

We continue our walk. And just like that, Mum seems to become preoccupied and a little apprehensive. I can feel it in the space between us, and in the way she moves – tentative and unsure.

There are no clues to tell her where we are and why we are here. Before I have time to remind her, she starts to ask questions. She has forgotten our little plan for today and is wondering where my dad is, she is keen to know if we are going to meet anyone, and, crucially, if there are any expectations of her. I remind her what we are doing and take the opportunity to say that she had suggested we go out for a walk so we can spend some time together and Dad can get on with his jobs for the day. For a very short time this reassures her, but then she asks again and again. I give her the clarity she needs and try to develop and redirect the conversation. All my attempts bring us back to the same questions, where are we going, where is Guy, etc. When I say that we are giving Dad a bit of time to himself, without thinking I use the word *break*, this leads to her becoming concerned that he needs a break from her, that he doesn't want her around anymore because she drives him mad with all her questions. I tell her that this just isn't true, and only yesterday he said she was the love of his life. She wavers for a moment, taking this on board.

I spot an ice cream van along the seafront, always a great opportunity to shift the focus. "I don't know about you, but I fancy an ice cream!" The cycle is broken, and we decide to have an ice cream and not tell Dad or Simon. She loves this kind of secret agreement, although if she remembers she will be the first to tell our other halves when we get home.

We sit on a bench licking our 99s and crunching our lovely chocolate flakes. Once again taking in the nature around us, we are now watching a flock of starlings doing their thing in unison. I tell her it's called a murmuration, and then with my very limited knowledge I try to describe how it works: each bird just being aware of the seven birds around them and using them as a guide, who are in turn just aware of the seven birds around them, and so on, which results in this spectacle of hundreds or even thousands of birds all moving together, as if they are one conscious being.

She lets me finish and then completely disregards my questionable comments and says, "You see all those birds moving in the sky together?"

"Yes," I reply.

"Who do you think taught them to do that?"

I know what's coming, but I say, "I don't know."

"God did." She says this in a tone that is in a large font, bold, underlined, and with a full stop. So, it's now clear that hers is the final comment on the subject, and the truth has been established.

Mum and I have just had one of many science-versus-religion discussions, and she has won by virtue of her unwavering belief. Her explanation was simpler and easier to understand than mine.

God works in mysterious ways.

* * *

Somebody on the next bench along decides to throw a couple of chips to the gulls. Suddenly it's chaos – the word has gone out and every gull within a ten-mile radius seems to be mobbing this poor man. I say to Mum, "Be careful what you wish for; he just wanted to be kind to a couple of gulls and now he has their extended family to contend with, and they don't seem to be taking no for an answer."

"So," I say, "the moral of the story is that it's best not to feed the birds."

Mum agrees, but, always the rule breaker, throws the remainder of her ice cream cone onto the ground in front of us. The birds react immediately, and we make a quick escape.

Heading back towards the car park, we see that the crow is no longer alone and is now with a large group of friends picking through some stranded seaweed. Seeing my chance to re-establish just a little credibility, I tell Mum something that I know is fact: "Did you know that when crows are in a group like that (pointing to the birds), they are known as a murder of crows?" She doesn't respond. Just gives me a sideways look that says it all.

"I imagine it was God that came up with that name," I add. She agrees, and we walk on.

We arrive home full of stories of babies, ice cream, crows and murder.

Being out in nature has done us both good.

Hearing Voices and Smelling Roses

Part of my dealing with Mum's condition is to find opportunities to openly talk about it to other people outside of our immediate family and friends. Simon and I haven't got a large social circle, and so I just speak about it if I feel it is OK to do so and there isn't a risk of unloading my concerns onto other people. I just need to be able to introduce the subject occasionally and share the headlines. This enables me to process and normalise things for myself.

A few days after our walk along the seafront, I bumped into a work colleague. We weren't particularly close, but we did have common ground, particularly a love of wildlife and nature, so when our paths occasionally crossed, we were able to have an enjoyable and interesting conversation, which I always came away from with a spring in my step and a plan to buy another bird feeder.

On this day we got onto talking about our parents, and I dropped into the conversation that my mum, who also loves nature, was living with dementia. I didn't introduce this as a subject that needed exploring, just as a kind of context setting so I could make a point about how being outside and connecting to wildlife clearly benefits her wellbeing and quality of life.

However, when I said this, my colleague's response really took me by surprise. Her tone became very serious, and her expression hardened. She had a very clear view of people living with dementia, and a solid and limiting opinion on what their life would, or even should, be like. I assumed she had experienced the illness in a family member or friend, and her comments and views were coming from somewhere personal, emotive, and upsetting.

It soon became obvious that I had made a mistake introducing this subject with this individual, and that I had inadvertently opened some raw emotions in her that, despite my best efforts, I could not steer her away from. Whatever her experience had been, she was determined to project her views onto my own, she was going to say what she felt she needed to, and that was the end of it.

There followed a good twenty minutes of one-way monologue that seemed to be focused on challenging and undermining any positive view of the dementia experience. For example, her instant response to my comment about being out in nature was that any perceived benefits were probably in my head to make me feel better about myself, as opposed to benefiting my mum in any way.

She went on to say that there was no value in doing something that would be instantly forgotten and, most shocking, that people with dementia are just as happy staring at the wallpaper. She had lots more to say, but I won't go into detail here, as the point of this book is to give an alternative perspective on living with the illness, by exploring opportunities for connection and belonging even if for fleeting moments in time.

I must point out that I don't think there were any bad intentions here, but these comments did influence my thinking on two levels: First, there was the initial shock that anybody would consider bursting my happy bubble, however misguided they may have thought I was! The second, and more profound, was that rather than having a negative impact on me, as I would expect, they made me acutely aware that if that alternative narrative is the one we chose to live by, then all potential and possibility of us continuing to live well with Mum's illness would be stripped out of the equation from this moment forwards.

This was powerful stuff. By exposing me to these opinions, my colleague had pushed me into the realisation that we all have a responsibility to choose to adopt and maintain an open mind and, in doing so, create an environment that enables people to flourish, grow and enjoy each moment as best they can. But this is a choice.

This person was telling my mum's story before it had been written, dismissing her right and ability to enjoy life; in fact, she was almost dismissing her as a valid human being. It was a shock to me personally, but I realised that this wasn't out of the ordinary, and it wasn't a personal attack. The truth is that society, and the media, tell this same limited and limiting story every day, and we owe it to our loved ones to come from a different place and to give them the space to belong, feel valued and maybe even to have some fun, even if it is just for the occasional fleeting moment.

This conversation was not about my mum; it was about me, and it acted as a catalyst – forcing me to really hear another viewpoint, one I wasn't comfortable with. And it made me question my beliefs and agenda:

Do I really believe that life can be meaningful despite this illness?

Yes, most definitely. In fact, in my mum's case it is the norm as opposed to a rarity.

Am I just feeding my ego and my need to make everything OK and come to the rescue?

Yes probably, on some level there are elements of this; don't we all have a desire to 'look after' our loved ones and save the day? Is that so terrible? Or rare?

Do I believe that having a growth mindset, focusing on strengths and opportunity, can positively impact on the way my mum and other people living with dementia experience the illness?

Yes – undoubtedly – there is no question.

So, what did I learn from this conversation? That sometimes it's useful to open your eyes, ears and mind to challenging, uncomfortable and opposing opinions to your own. This enables you to explore your own beliefs, motives, and values – which can be incredibly empowering. But be warned, only listen to those kinds of opinions if you are feeling resilient – if there is no space for it, don't go there. Your wellbeing is important, so take care of yourself. You know what is right for you. Live your life in the way you want to live it and be there for the people you care about.

In addition to this, make time to stop and smell the roses, check out the starlings...break a few rules...and maybe even feed ice cream to the seagulls.

Orange Crush on Jaywick Sands

Things are going well. It's early August, three months in, and Mum is really settling into her new house and has enjoyed being fully involved in turning it into a home. Today, however, she became upset and frustrated about going to the hairdressers, and I can understand why.

For many years she has had a weekly appointment on a Thursday morning in a hairdresser's where everyone knows her, and the salon, conveniently, is just around the corner from home. In preparation for this event, she will ensure she has enough money in her purse to pay for her hairdo plus a tip. She will check the time of the appointment, which is written on her calendar, then she will check she has a carrier bag in her handbag in case she buys anything in the corner shop on her way back. This ritual may start several days before the appointment and will usually be repeated many times. Not relying totally on her calendar and clock, she will also check the details with my dad. Repeating the same questions, going into the kitchen to check the calendar, and then once again checking with my dad. Sometimes this cycle can be broken by a change of subject or redirecting her attention to something else. But at other times it continues.

When the time for the much-anticipated appointment finally arrives, she will set off and walk to the salon, which includes crossing two roads, one of which is busy, but there are traffic lights, so she presses the button. When she arrives, she will be greeted by name by the fantastic staff, she will chat, laugh, tell stories, and listen to what is being said, and maybe even get a cup of tea. After the appointment she will walk back home, often popping into the corner shop on the way to say hello and probably buy something.

This regular event is yet another example of my dad's natural approach to positive risk-taking and his deep love for his wife. Let's face it, he could walk her to the hairdressers and collect her afterwards; that would be far easier and risk-free. But going alone gives her a real sense of independence and usually results in her arriving home looking good with her freshly done hair and feeling proud of herself for not needing any help. She will often also be carrying a newspaper, a carton of milk or a packet of biscuits from the shop – she always has been and will always be the provider. I say usually, because, just like her solo dog walking adventures, now and again things do not quite go to plan. For example, there have been times when she has returned from a dog walk with no dog, or the dog has arrived home with no walker. Likewise, once or twice she has turned the wrong way when leaving the hairdresser's and headed off towards the fire station. But these small events have always been resolved with little drama; the key is not to overreact and knock her confidence. My dad rightly believes that the benefits and notion of self-worth Mum experiences because of her independent activities far outweigh the likelihood of any harm occurring.

As time, and my mum's condition, have progressed, Dad has had to add unintrusive safety measures. For example, in the last couple of years he has walked with her as far as the road crossing, in order for him to go to the bakers to buy bread, but also ensuring she crosses the road safely. He has also arranged that the hairdresser will phone him when Mum is leaving, and he will walk around and meet her halfway. Road safety is one of those *ingrained* things that she has not lost at all, but there are two people involved here, and my dad also needs to feel confident and reassured that all is well. The great thing about these extra measures is that they reflect and support her changing needs but still stick to the core principles of independent living and positive risk-taking.

But now this routine, along with many others, has changed. Mum is going to a different hairdresser. My dad has arranged that the appointment is still on a Thursday, which is great because having her hair done is the predominant milestone she uses to monitor her way through the week. The layout of the new salon is similar to the previous one, as is the smell, the offer of a cup of tea, and the friendly and relaxed atmosphere. So, things are pretty good. But the downside to this new arrangement is that being farther away from home, and in unknown territory, my dad now drives her to the appointment. This does not bode well with Mum's independent spirit, but there is a kind of compromise, which is that he drops her off along the road, so she walks by herself and pays out of her purse, etc. It's so important to her that she is seen by the people at the salon as the self-reliant woman that she has always been.

Being a Thursday, this morning she got up early, washed, dressed and was all ready to go when there was a call from the salon explaining there had been some kind of mix up with bookings and, full of apologies, they had rescheduled her appointment to tomorrow. Not really a big deal on the face of it.

But it has resulted in a repeated cycle of questions, answers, and frustrations as Mum gets the information she needs but then doesn't seem to be able to retain it. However many times I try to explain what is happening, it's just not helping. In fact, I think she is finding my reassuring *good son* tone decidedly aggravating.

We sit and I listen to her concerns. I need to stop looking for solutions until she is ready. It's not that it's inconvenient or anything like that; it's just the confusion that this change has triggered. It's as if she was holding a deck of cards that have been put in order, with all the facts she needs to have some sense of control, and then suddenly somebody throws them all up in the air and the resulting muddle is overwhelming. I listen and give her some space and time to air her frustrations. All she really wants is the plan – "So what's happening now?" Together, we write the new appointment time and details on her whiteboard in the lounge.

* * *

Now she is feeling a little more settled, I try to redirect her attention and suggest we head down the garden to the garage for a cup of tea. She laughs. "Who goes into their garage for a cup of tea!?"

And here we are, drama sorted, sitting on armchairs in the little wooden garage Simon and I built at the end of our garden inspired by all those huts and cabins in Wrabness. I call it a garage, but it's more than that. It houses our campervan, but it also has furniture and a wood burner – the point being we can camp in our van whenever we want. It sounds ridiculous, but it's wonderful.

I put the kettle on, and we sit looking at a colour photograph taken more than fifty years ago. The picture is small, square, and shiny with a white border. It is a little tatty around the edges and has evidence of some kind of glue on the back where it has either been stuck into a frame or maybe a photo album. It has a musty smell to it, which is a remnant of its most recent place of residence – an old suitcase of letters, photos, and dusty plane tickets I found under the bed in the spare room.

The picture is dominated by a small flight of wooden steps with a handrail leading up to the open door of a small wooden chalet-style cabin. At the bottom of the steps is a path on top of a thick, curved concrete sea wall. At the top of the steps, just outside the doorway is my mum's mum, Flo, my nan. She is wearing a brown and cream summer dress and a pearl necklace. She has the look of the seaside about her. Whenever I think of Nan, I see her indoors. In fact, I see her standing in her little kitchen in Bengeo. Any outdoor photographs of her are taken on family holidays, and to be honest, she never looks completely relaxed. It's all a bit fish out of water. In this picture the wind has caught her hair, and the sun is making her squint. From her stance and expression, it's clear that sandy steps are not her natural habitat, and she is holding firmly onto the handrail. However, she is smiling at the photographer.

Halfway down the steps and leaning back confidently on the opposite handrail is my mum. Dark, wavy hair pushed back behind her ears. Fifties-style *cat-eye* glasses with those little wings lifting the top outside edge of each lens. She is wearing a pale yellow cardigan over a green and cream flared dress that, like Flo's, is also being blown about by the breeze. She looks happy and relaxed. With her two young boys standing either side of her, she is a proud and beautiful mother. Martin, who is to her right, has blond hair, a blue T-shirt, blue shorts, and bare feet. I hate to say it, but he is undoubtedly the cute one. I am on her left and have wriggled my way in close, so I am leaning the side of my head onto her hip. She is resting her hand on my left shoulder. I have short, dark hair, a gappy grin and am clearly a little dazzled by the sun in my eyes. I'm wearing the same blue shorts as Martin, a yellow top, and red sandals with a small buckle. I am about six.

Judging by the smile on my mum's face, I am assuming my dad is the man behind the lens.

Recognising the little wooden chalet on stilts, we both agree it must be Jaywick Sands in Essex, on the east coast of England. This small building had a big influence on me, at that very early age. I'm not sure if it was the dimensions and shape, the stilts it stood on, or its uncanny resemblance to the house the Swiss Family Robinson built on their island. But whatever the reason, I fell in love with it, and its memory has occupied a tiny corner in my heart ever since.

Jaywick was the number one holiday destination for our young family for several years, and this photograph has triggered memories for both of us. Mum is now telling me all about those magical holidays and speaks as if she very clearly remembers the moment the photograph was taken – and maybe she does. She speaks as if it is happening right now. She says that her dad is in the chalet listening to the horse racing on the radio; his wife is annoyed with him as he is refusing to come out into the sunshine, hence that look on her face that I mistook for a sun-dazzled squint. Our cousin Zena, who usually came on these annual holidays with us, is not in the picture, but Mum, stepping outside of its white borders, says that Zena is on the beach decorating our sandcastle with flags and shells.

She goes on to explain that we went to Jaywick because it was just about affordable and was close to home, so the journey wasn't too long for us kids. Although I know this is true and it was only about fifty miles door to door, I realise that my memory of those holidays includes a massive road trip at each end, which involved getting up before dawn and loading the car with everything we owned. Then, once on our way, we would need to stop at least three times for a wee, a Wagon Wheel, some fresh air, and a plastic cup of sweet tea from a flask. Surely not all of this in just fifty miles? Maybe my memories are muddled and I'm confusing this with later, more daring holidays when we travelled further afield.

I realise that Mum has now forgotten the hairdressers, her worries have drained away and she is dipping her toes into the salty sea off the coast of Essex. She says that when we paddled, Martin would look for crabs in rock pools while I collected shells to take back to the cabin on stilts. At dusk we would all sit on the sea wall and eat fish and chips. It sounds idyllic, and it was. She then says that after our fish and chips we would travel by tram back to where we were staying. Just like my hazy memory of the mammoth car journey, I realise her story is now shifting to a different family holiday and she is talking about a place we stayed in Devon a few years later. Enjoying our conversation, I join her on the tram and talk about the bird sanctuary it passed through and the cottage we stayed in with a stream running through the garden. Although, unlike my mum, I do not have a memory of this photograph being taken, I do have a very strong memory of a holiday in Jaywick, which I decide to add to the pot.

I ask her if she remembers the little Dancette record player we had at the bungalow in Roydon, and she says that she does. It was orange and beige, and it could stack up to seven 45RPM singles at a time. As each record finished, a magical sequence of complex mechanical movements was triggered, culminating in the tone arm lowering onto the next disc. As the stack on the turntable grew taller, the stack hovering above it waiting to be played got smaller. My favourite record of the stack was "White Horses" by Jackie; I think it was the theme to some TV show. My brother liked "Double Barrel" by Dave and Ansell Collins. My dad's favourite was "If Not for You" by the lovely Olivia Newton John, and my mum's was "The Twelfth of Never" by Johnny Mathis.

The Dancette, which was portable, had a hinged lid with catches to fasten it closed, and a handle on the side so it could be carried like a suitcase. My memory tells me we took it with us on holiday to Jaywick Sands. Nobody else in the family has any memory of this, and it is almost definitely not fact. But as we know, memory is fickle, and I have clearly created my own truth here. However, as we sit in the garage chatting over the photograph, my mum is completely up for remembering the record player being taken on holiday and even elaborates by mentioning my dad playing his Ella Fitzgerald record in the evening. God, how I love talking to this woman – we can just create our own realities whenever we want, and we never correct each other!

Once Ella has been introduced to the conversation, I can't resist telling my often-repeated bad joke, which, of course, my mum is hearing for the first time: "Mum, you know Ella Fitzgerald was married, don't you?"

"Yes," she answers seriously.

"Do you know her husband's name?" I ask.

"No, I can't think who her husband was – your dad would know," she says, with real curiosity in her voice.

"Ella Fitzgerald's husband was called Gerald Fitz-Ella – they were the perfect fit!" The penny drops and she is laughing out loud.

"You *are* daft," she says through giggles.

"It's true!" I exclaim...

So here I am creating my own truth about the record player and repeating myself while assuming people are hearing my joke for the first time. And my mum is joining me in my truth – she is with me in the moment. Just like Gerald and Ella, we are a perfect fit.

I'm now telling her that I remember the chalet as being very cosy with two or three small rooms. The floors were covered by patterned lino, which I suppose was easy to sweep as we, and all the other lucky visitors, traipsed in and out with sandy feet. It seemed to my young eyes to be the perfect home, and I have never forgotten it. In fact, I don't think the building we are sitting in now at the end of my garden would exist if I hadn't been so bewitched by my childhood adventures on the east coast of England in a tiny magical house on stilts.

I ask if she thinks Zena would have bought her favourite record to Jaywick. Instantly she says, "Yes, of course she did! And it was 'Congratulations' by Cliff Richard!"

I agree. "Zena wouldn't go anywhere without Cliff."

It's wonderful that, despite the frustration she felt just half an hour ago, she is now chatting and laughing and can instantly recall that Zena always has been a huge Cliff fan and loves "Congratulations." I notice that Mum and I are working collaboratively to create this story, playing off each other's comments to add the details and fill in any gaps. I am also noticing that we are not just making any of this up. Every detail is based on something that happened at some point, on some holiday. Or on the things that we know about individuals. For example, Zena's obsession with Cliff.

I am now talking about Carny the Labrador; he must have been with us at Jaywick, and there is no doubt he would have been indulging in his favourite pastime – passing wind in confined spaces, so that would have added to the atmosphere in our compact little holiday home; on reflection, maybe that is why we stopped so many times on our fifty-mile car trip. My mum starts laughing when I say this and is now wondering if that's why Flo's smile is a borderline grimace. Although she has been my mum for over fifty years, I still refrain from saying anything 'rude' in front of her and feel a bit naughty if I do. I'm thinking that a dog fart from fifty years ago is just about acceptable.

* * *

Jaywick Sands was built in the 1930s as a holiday resort for people from the East End of London. It had a little fun fair called Wonderland, a gift shop, and a clubhouse. To me, Jaywick was paradise – no school, a house on stilts, a bucket and spade and (crucially) a pack of sandcastle flags – what more could I want? I tell my mum that it was in Wonderland that I had my first real crush. She is a little surprised at this intimate subject change, but also curious to know more.

He was driving one of the mini dodgems, and we crashed into each other under sparks of electricity. He was older than me – maybe seven or eight – he had blond hair, wore a Dennis the Menace T-shirt and was drinking Fanta Orange. He was amazing. I remembered my mum describing Johnny Mathis as "*so…international.*" I didn't know what that meant (still don't), but I was pretty sure my new friend was just that.

The dodgems cost sixpence a go, so I asked Nan for money, telling her that I wanted to go on the Dumbo ride. However, in reality, I was going to the dodgems to treat my new friend to a ride. My six-year-old mind told me that the way to a man's heart was to pay for him in Wonderland. He would swig his Fanta Orange from a bottle while buzzing around laughing and smiling at me. My memory tells me that as he did this, Jackie was singing "White Horses" through little tinny speakers hanging above the dodgems.

Mum wants to hear the song – and through the wonders of technology, within seconds I have found it on the internet. Then as we chat, I play the other songs we have mentioned and some additional tracks that have come to mind.

While we listen, I tell her that I wanted life on the dodgems with my new friend to go on forever. We would live together in a wooden chalet on stilts overlooking the sea, and we'd spend our time in Wonderland going on rides and drinking Fanta Orange. I love how she is taking this all in her stride and clearly understands the way my young mind was working.

I'm not sure if I was aware that my plans for our life together were different to the norm; I was too young to understand that kind of thing. I do know that what I felt, and was hoping for, came from the heart. Looking back, I'm pretty sure the whole thing was one-sided – I hadn't mentioned my plans to him.

Day after day, we played together on the beach, in Wonderland or sneaking around under chalets. Then one morning he casually mentioned he was going home that afternoon – and he did.

I visited the dodgems in hope, but he was gone. It's sad to think about, even now.

That was my first solid memory of being a (very young) gay man – except that's not what we were called back then.

I have never shared this story with Mum before and haven't really talked openly to her about being gay. Obviously, she knows I am, and she loves Simon, but I have never spoken about it like this. But she just operates in a world of love. She clearly identifies with the emotion of the story that I am describing, even if it is the experience of a six-year-old kid. She goes on to tell me about when she met my dad. It really was love at first sight. She worried that when he went home, he may never come back again. Despite having only been together for a short time, she just couldn't imagine a life without him.

I then tell her about when myself and Simon first met. I was planning to leave the area and most probably head back to a life in Australia. I met him, I felt a real connection, but should I change my plans based on a hunch? Well, I did, and twenty-six years later here I am telling her about it. She says she loves Simon even more now she knows he stopped me leaving the country.

She looks at the photograph as if for the first time. "Where is that?... It must be Jaywick... Look at my hair!"

Then she asks, "When is my hair appointment?"

As we get up to leave the garage, Mum is looking inside our campervan, and she tells me that it smells familiar, and it reminds her of that heady cocktail of engine oil, cooking, and polish that lingered halfway up the stairs of 1 Parker Avenue. We climb in the van and sit down facing each other. The hair appointment is forgotten once more and, although the two vehicles could not be more different, we are now sitting in the Rolls Royce that my grandad occasionally collected his two young daughters from school in, setting the teacher's hearts fluttering. This then leads to emotions being triggered, misplaced memories rediscovered, and as we sit in a little green van, in a cabin at the end of the garden, new stories being told.

A Falcon for a Nave

In the interest of making the most of this beautiful summer's day, and for my parents to get to know the local area, we are heading to Chichester to have a walk around the Roman Wall and find somewhere to have lunch. But there is a problem. This is a plan without detail, and that, for my mum, is an unwelcome business, fraught with potentially risky events. So, to be frank – she's not interested.

Even as we pass Arundel Castle, which stands grand and proud on the edge of a valley in the South Downs, she keeps a long face and hardly even acknowledges it. This is so out of character because, like her youngest son, she is a great talker, even if nobody is listening. And a magnificent eleventh-century castle with towers, turrets and flags is just the kind of thing that would normally get her attention. So, as we continue our journey, I reflect that she must be very determined not to enjoy herself, and that this is probably going to be a tough day.

There are three very good reasons for us to be heading to Chichester: 1) There is a beautiful cathedral with glorious stained-glass windows, which I know my mum will love; 2) living up high in the turrets of the cathedral's spire is a family of peregrine falcons, two adults and two youngsters, which I know my dad will be fascinated by due to his life-long love of birds; and 3) Chichester is a great place for people watching, a family pastime, which is always entertaining. Each of these attractions is very much an *in the moment activity* – something that cannot be impeded by dementia. Thinking about all this, I tell myself it's worth it.

The warm sun shines down on us as we walk through a park and into the city centre. We are heading for the Cathedral Café to have a drink, look through our binoculars, and watch the live cam of the beautiful falcons nesting and hunting up high above. On the way to the café, we pass the main door to the cathedral, and we hear the magical sounds of a choir rehearsing. On noticing this, Mum stops dead in her tracks, her mood lifts and she tells us to be quiet and listen. It is a haunting and emotive sound; its purpose is to make our spirits soar – which even from outside the building it certainly does. Mum and I decide to go inside while our other halves continue their pilgrimage to the peregrines.

On entering the cathedral, its size and scale is almost overwhelming. It is huge, peaceful, and otherworldly. The choir is still singing, almost chanting, hidden away in the cloisters, somewhere unseen. As we wander around the nave, I notice my mum carries herself with a certain respectful reverence, and that for the first time today she looks relaxed. She is in awe of her surroundings, taking it all in, right now in the moment. No comments about people's shoes, or questions about where we are; she just has an air of contentment and comfort in a very familiar setting, but one that we have never visited before. We sit down in a pew as there is lots to see and to listen to, and probably to contemplate.

After a while, Mum turns to me and quietly says, "It's funny, whenever you go into a church, wherever it is in the world, it always smells the same, and it's not a smell you get in any other building." I think about what she has said and agree; it is true.

Then she adds, "And do you know what the smell is?" Before I have time to think, she says, "It's the Holy Spirit," and smiles.

She is calm, there is no anxiety, and she is content at just being here. Her concerns and mild anger have fallen away.

As we sit and soak up the atmosphere, in hushed tones, she then tells me a story I have never heard before. During the war, she, her mum, and her sister Sylvia were walking to church on a Sunday morning, when they passed a house that had been damaged in an air raid. There was a woman, searching through the rubble and debris, collecting any belongings that could be salvaged. Flo called her name, she glanced up with a look of grief, loss and despair in her eyes, and then they greeted each other with a smile, behaving in an ordinary way despite the extraordinary and devastating situation. It was clear that the woman was in a desperate situation. She went on to say something else, but before she could speak, her eyes lit up and she exclaimed, "Trixie, thank God!" A little cat had appeared through the rubble and dust. The woman gathered her up in her arms with tears in her eyes.

Amid all this destruction, she was overjoyed that her little pet had survived. Mum then says that the woman must have prayed to God for the life of her little companion, and he had answered her prayers. We are both moved by this story. For me it is the woman clambering around amongst the destruction with a look of loss on her face being suddenly moved to tears by the appearance of her friend. For my mum it was the assumption that Trixie's survival must have been due to God answering her prayers. It's all the proof she needs, and her faith is infectious. We both sit and reflect and thank God for sparing Trixie.

After a few minutes of silence, she turns to me and says that being in this building reminds her of her mum, and she tells me some more snippets of stories. I can recognise an emotional tone in her voice and can see her eyes have moistened. I mention that my memory of her mum, my nan, is a smell that I can't put a name to, but still every now and again it lands on my senses, and I think of Flo.

Straight away, my mum says, "That's Pond's Cold Cream!"

"She used it all the time; ask my sister, she'll tell you all about it."

She continues, "When we were kids, we used to sneak in her room and steal little dabs of it."

I marvel at her ability to remember the name of my nan's favourite face cream thirty-five years after her death, but that she has forgotten that her sister who she was so close to for over eighty years passed away six years ago. Of course, I don't remind her about this; why would I? I just thank her for telling me the name of the mystery smell – which she enjoys.

We decide to light a small tea-light at the altar for Flo and Trixie.

Just walking into this building and soaking up the atmosphere has had a profound and positive effect on Mum. This multi-sensory experience has provided a conduit for her to connect, not only with memories of the past, but also with a higher and familiar sense of peace and wellbeing. It occurs to me that what she said was right – this environment, with all its reassuring spiritual energy and ambiance, can be found in almost any town or village all over the world. For the first time in my life, I realise that for people of faith, when they step into a place of worship, they are also stepping into a place of familiar strength, safety, reassurance and, crucially, belonging. What a gift!

We leave the cathedral and look at the gargoyles up high on the outside of the building. One catches our attention. It is a man wearing glasses who looks remarkably like my Uncle Les, Mum's brother-in-law. In truth the gargoyle depicts Clifford Hodgetts, the former registrar to the dean and chapter of the cathedral. But the fact remains that if Uncle Les ever donned a curly wig, and we have no evidence that he ever did or did not, then he would be the spitting image of Mr. Hodgetts and the gargoyle. This moment of comedy lightens both of our moods, and we spend a few minutes matching the looks and characteristics of other Chichester gargoyles to family and friends.

We find our other halves in the Cathedral Café. Having been chatting to a raptor expert, they are full of peregrine falcon facts. Peregrines are the fastest animal on earth, diving at speeds of up to 240 miles per hour. They can see small prey up to two miles away, and they choose to nest on high cliffs and buildings, which is why they return to Chichester Cathedral every year. Lots has happened in the last thirty minutes; Mum has walked into a building feeling anxious and disconnected, and walked out again feeling in touch, grounded and with a big smile on her face. I have experienced a little glimpse of, and a connection with, a more spiritual side of life that I haven't really thought about for a very long time, and we have both given thanks for the life of the little cat with only eight remaining lives, and for the great Florence Meeks, without whom none of us would be sitting here today.

Meanwhile, my dad and Simon have also been moved, but they were moved by the grace, beauty and agility of the peregrine falcon, although I must say that the colourful and brutal language they used to describe the fate of the pigeons they prey on bought us all crashing back down to earth from our dizzy spiritual heights.

A little later we buy a jar of Pond's Cold Cream, which like Aladdin's lamp contains magical aromas, long-lost memories, and new stories.

The Sea, the Rescue, and What Lurks Beneath

Work has been a struggle today. I managed, unintentionally, to upset somebody, and then in my eagerness to make amends, I just made things worse. When I got home, I went around to see Mum and dad which, just a few months since the move, has already become a good remedy if some cheering up is needed. But unfortunately, instead of adjusting my mindset, I jumped straight in and took my dark mood with me. Before I knew it, without thinking, I had been snappy with them. So, I decide it's best if I just step away from people for a while and dip my toes into the natural world, and here I am cycling down to the seafront for a splash in the sea, which should help me get my head around everything that has happened and crucially get things in perspective.

I am swimming. It's September, autumn is on its way and the waves are big and powerful, and as the tide is turning, the current is strong enough to pull me in the opposite direction to what I intended. On entering the water, I experienced the familiar, expected, but strangely still shocking moment as the dark, cold water came into contact with my skin. I stepped forwards gingerly, as the water made its way up my legs and my toes grappled with the rocks, stones, and plants beneath the surface. I jumped up as waves approached, trying to minimise the shock. But then I did what was needed and lunged forwards into the surf; I gasped for breath for a few long slow-motion seconds, before my moving limbs created some warmth, which, again, happened surprisingly quickly.

A few minutes later I have acclimatised, and I float on my back, limbs outstretched and moving gently with slow, deep breaths. If I were in snow, I would be creating angels with my arms and legs. I pull my goggles up onto my forehead so I can clearly see the clouds and gulls high above, as the sea laps around my face. My relaxed body is rising, falling, drifting, and turning with the swell and currents. I suppose you could say I am giving in to the sea and trusting my body to look after me. It still amazes me that the delicate balance between the weight of my body and that of the water it has displaced results in me being able to float with my eyes, nose, and mouth just above the surface. I momentarily stifle a panic as I think about the unimaginable power of the ocean being held in check by simple physics.

The sensual and emotional experience of being physically connected and almost a part of my immediate environment is all-consuming and liberating. Not just the water, air and power, but also the smell and taste of the sea, the sound of stones being pushed and drawn, the crashing of waves, and the call of the gulls. It's both highly chaotic and incredibly familiar and predictable.

As I reflect on this, I also draw some alignment with what my mum described when we were in Chichester Cathedral – feeling a part of the environment and a connection to a greater, all-consuming, and redeeming power.

I think about our mantra, *With You in the Moment*, and realise that being totally present, as things are happening, isn't just a good rule of thumb when I am interacting with her; maybe I also need to consciously apply it when I'm interacting with the world I live in and the life I am trying to lead. Stop waiting for the future and live life to the full, as it happens. I am feeling very positive and am enjoying flowing with the power of the sea rather than fighting it. I decide that from now on I need to literally go with the flow more often; then I can focus my energy on the important things in life.

This experience is multi-layered, or maybe multi-functional. It not only raises my awareness of the here and now but also connects me with other moments from the timeline of my life. Right now, my brain is sparking connections between my present senses and recollections of similar experiences from the past.

* * *

I am thinking about a very significant time when I was travelling in Australia. I was young with few responsibilities, hitchhiking my way up the east coast with everything I needed in my backpack. I was meeting new people, reading great books and having interesting conversations. And all this taking place in, under, or beside the Pacific Ocean. My memories of this time are of great warmth and revelation for me, with fleeting moments of complete freedom and feelings of physical and spiritual confidence.

This was the first time in my life that I had felt comfortable in my body, and able to be my true self in front of other people. I was curious about everything, open to ideas and I had a new kind of self-respect and awareness that enabled me to absorb and learn in a way that had never happened in my early life or at school. Those few months of swimming, talking, reading, and running gave me not only a physical confidence but also a feeling that my thoughts, ideas and opinions had as much value as anyone else's and, despite what I was told at school, I was able to learn and contribute.

Although those events were profound at the time and played a part in shaping the person I have become in later life, it is fair to say that I haven't really thought about them in this way for a long time. So, there is no doubt in my mind that my present sensory experience of swimming on the south coast of England has triggered connections with experiences that took place over thirty-five years ago on the other side of the world. The amazing thing is that this is much more than just looking back on a past event. I feel directly in touch with my younger self, and my mind and body are once again alive and tingling with feelings of health, and wellbeing. I am reconnecting with feelings of self-worth and value that have often deserted me in adult life. I feel good.

As the sun passes behind a cloud and brings a giant shadow racing across the surface of the sea, there is a slight reduction in light, and my brain tricks me into thinking the temperature of the water has suddenly dropped. As a result of this I feel an imagined chill, which triggers a real shiver of goosebumps throughout my body and a slight feeling of threat.

The tendrils in my brain gently let go of the joys of Australia and the Tropic of Capricorn and are now connecting to the murky river next to our little bungalow in Essex. As kids we would swim from bank to bank, jump off the concrete bridge, or float around on inflated lorry inner tubes. The water was a milky dark green soup, the banks were slippery, and the river bottom was sinking mud, which felt like it could drag you down into the world of unseen dangers such as crayfish and pike.

This was a popular place for fishing, and the gruesome remains of caught and gutted creatures on the riverbank served to remind us that there were hidden live ones below the surface with sharp teeth and vise-like claws. I can remember the earthy taste of the water and the smell of decomposing vegetation mixed with inner tube rubber. I can also remember my mad, panicky scramble every time my legs brushed against something lurking in the depths, or my feet sunk into the bottomless silky sludge of the riverbed.

As I continue to float, this memory makes me instantly and acutely aware of unlikely dangers; those twitchy insecurities from years gone by reignite in my nervous system, and in an instant I am alert and questioning – what lurks beneath?

Then something brushes past my calf. Or I think it did. *Shit! What was that?* My goosebumps are invigorated, and I am on high alert. I control my impulse to turn onto my front and head for shore – but, just in case, I do a quick scan for dorsal fins. Not a common occurrence in Sussex, but worth checking just in case. The confident side of my personality plays the theme from *Jaws*, just to ridicule the insecure side.

To redirect my thinking and to dilute my fears, I raise my head and take in my dynamic surroundings. The stony beach, the rocky breakwaters and, in the distance, the amazing Art Deco pier reaching out into the watery wilderness in a desperate attempt to tame the untameable. My towel and bag are about one hundred and fifty metres west of where I expect them to be, so the current is obviously stronger than I realise. I begin to swim my weird version of breaststroke, heading towards my gear and against the current. I say weird because I have never really understood what I'm supposed to be doing with my legs, so they kind of flail and flap along behind me, like the tentacles of a jellyfish, more a hindrance than help. I'm not sure I'm making any progress. This feeling of being carried against my will by a force far greater than I can overcome then triggers another memory, but this time it is somebody else's and it took place in this very stretch of water.

I'm thinking about Simon and his first bash at kitesurfing. At the time kitesurfing was a relatively new sport with few participants. I think it was already taking a hold in the West Country and possibly overseas, but it was almost unheard of in our part of the world. Simon, wanting to learn without an audience, was in the sea alone. He had been watching videos and reading magazines to understand how to find the tension between sea and wind power and to find out more about technique. He was already a very experienced and skilled kite flyer and had been using power kites for several years.

On this particular occasion he'd launched the kite on the beach, paddled out on his board behind the breakers and found the *wind window*, which is the area of sky that gives the kite the most power. He was feeling good; his mind and body were in the moment and were responding to both wind and wave. This was great, and he was gaining confidence as he raced across the water skimming the peaks of each wave. He was standing up and leaning back, finding equilibrium between air, water, and forward motion.

Then suddenly, a strong and unexpected gust from a new direction. With a jolt, the kite flipped and crashed onto the water, crossing its lines and making it near impossible for him to relaunch. The kite, finding stability on its inflatable edge, captured the full force of the wind in its sail, and in a split second Simon found himself being dragged out to sea. As he struggled and repeatedly failed to take control, a dark feeling of fear grew in his chest and, despite the chaos, he started to weigh up his options. The safest and most obvious thing to do was free himself, from what was now a very powerful drag, by unclipping the harness and detaching himself from the kite, then paddling back to shore on the board, which was attached to his ankle by a leash. However, despite his escalating panic and awareness of the very real danger he was facing, he couldn't contemplate giving up his beautiful new kite. So, illogically, he opted to just hold on tight and soon found himself in a desperate situation heading past the end of the pier and out to sea. The waves were growing angry, and the water, dark and more chaotic.

He later told me that as he was dragged uncontrollably towards the horizon, he started to instinctively holler my name, calling for me to come and rescue him. Thinking about this detail, his nonsensical but desperate call across the waves and time reminds me of the bond we have between us. I can hear his calling right now.

Of course, on the actual day of this incident, his hollering went unheard; I was miles away and well out of earshot, but having been spotted by somebody on the shore looking through their binoculars, he was instead rescued by the RNLI. This was very fortunate because they definitely had a head start on me when it came to saving lives at sea. He was shaken but OK, and so was his lovely kite, but unfortunately the following day the story and a picture appeared in a local newspaper, which bruised his pride a little.

Simon and I will always rescue each other from danger, and with this in mind I am once again floating on my back feeling safe and loved.

Looking towards the beach, I discover that my breaststroke was ineffective compared to the current and I have drifted further east and now I can't even see my gear. I soon realise that I have unwittingly passed a breakwater that juts out into the sea, and I am now looking at a different section of beach. I see a man and woman on a bank of shingle looking at me, and I feel a slight flush of embarrassment as they watch me swim in one direction while travelling in the opposite – a skill I acquired in Cyprus. I put more effort in and start to make progress.

Then I see a boy standing on the rocky breakwater gazing down into the crashing waves, and I realise the couple aren't looking at me at all – why would they! They are obviously the boy's parents, and they are now trying to get his attention by calling to him. But their words are lost in the cacophony of a billion tiny bubbles exploding onto the surface of the water. Then he glances their way, grinning to check they are watching him, but he is unaware of, or ignoring their calls and gesticulations.

This is so familiar, and once again I think about Simon. It was the mid-nineties, and one of our first days out as a couple. I suppose you could say it was a date. We went swimming together to a local pool with high diving boards. Being more of a daredevil than me, Simon had climbed up onto the top board, while I attempted to swim in the busy lanes preoccupied with not being crashed into by future Olympians or held back by two-abreast chattering lane hogs.

When I reached the end, I glanced up, assuming Simon was

no longer on the board and was now in the water. But there he was, hanging around with a weird look on his face. His hair didn't look wet, so I assumed maybe he wasn't as brave as he had made out. He caught my eye, waved, grinned, and moved to the edge of the board. Then I realised that he wasn't going to jump until he was sure I was watching. I waved and made it clear that I was indeed watching, and he immediately launched himself out into air and then water. Once he had done this and I was suitably impressed, he repeated the stunt again and again, each time being slightly more daring and each time checking my eyes were on him. He was wooing me with his bravery, and it worked. To be fair, I think I was also trying to impress him with my super slick lane swimming – but deep down I know it is neither super, nor slick, so I don't imagine he was wooed in any way.

Feeling immersed in this memory, I can smell the chlorinated water and hear the echoes of screams and laughter as they bounced from wall to wall, to the high ceiling of the indoor pool. I had completely forgotten about this event, but now I'm grinning from ear to ear, thinking about his innocent and basic need to be praised for what he could do by somebody who was important to him. Since that time, we have both spent hundreds of hours swimming up and down lanes looking at blue tiles and listening to bubbles being forced through the water by our strokes. Simon is a smooth, powerful and effortless swimmer; I am all arms and legs. Not pretty, but what I lack in style I make up for in determination. I look back towards the boy on the breakwater and catch the moment he leaps into the waves while his parents look on with admiration and probably a twinge of concern. He has his audience.

Back in the present moment, I become aware that the size of the waves is increasing, and feeling a chill, I pull my goggles back on and head for my gear on the beach. I glance at my watch and find I have only been floating around for about twenty minutes, but it feels like ages. It's amazing how my mind has made connections, and my chain of thought has taken me on a tour through a network of past experiences, projecting them into my consciousness in glorious technicolour with full sensory effects and emotions.

* * *

I tentatively walk up the stony beach to my gear and bike. And, once dry, sit in shorts and a gloriously warm and cosy hoodie, watching a small flock of gulls hang in the air, all facing the same direction. On the tideline, a murder of crows is picking at three dead dogfish that have washed up at regular intervals along the foamy border between water and land.

Stepping into this environment of present and past has left me feeling a strange combination of melancholy and excited possibility. If I had somebody with me, I would be sharing some of these recollections and telling them who I am, why swimming in the sea is part of my story and how the sound of waves crashing and gulls calling is an ever-present element of my life's soundtrack.

But maybe if I had somebody with me, I wouldn't have had the space to drift in body and spirit.

I think about my struggles from earlier today, my reasons for coming down to the sea in the first place, and I realise they haven't crossed my mind since my toes touched the water, and in the grand scheme of things they are insignificant. The swim has naturally pressed pause on what I was thinking and feeling. It has put a multi-sensory stopgap between then and now, and it has connected me with events that, I now realise, have resulted in my being able to see things more clearly. My challenges of this morning and their accompanying feeling of low self-worth have faded, and now my mood has lifted. I feel a kind of exhilaration and happiness. I will enjoy this feeling right now, in the moment, and avoid letting my mind drift off into any unhelpful reasons not to be cheerful.

I lay back on the stones and put my hands behind my

head, and I think about my mum. We are so similar. She links the present with the past and connects different experiences to events from her life as if they were just yesterday or even today, and these are the stories she likes to tell. These are the tales that can switch her mood in an instant, they can make her laugh or move her to tears, but crucially, remind her what an extraordinary life she has led and continues to lead.

I get it, and to be honest, I'm looking forward to getting home and telling Simon about my swim and the thoughts that it evoked – particularly the kitesurfing near-disaster. I will also pick up some chocolate and beer on the way home to remind Mum, Dad, and Simon that I love them.

I am beginning to understand the value of this kind of experience for somebody living with dementia. It's just a matter of ensuring people have the opportunity, time, and space to really be present in the moment and stop to take in the world round them. I am not saying that everyone living with this illness should bob about in the sea for an hour to connect with a deeper part of their being – unless that is one of the things that really makes them tick, of course, which it may well do; let's not make assumptions. What I'm saying is that any relevant experience in the here and now, whether it be hearing, tasting, smelling, touching, seeing or creating – all of these can build links that, if responded to by others with interest, curiosity and respect, can provide confidence and a sense of identity, pride, belonging and value: a portal to remind people who they really are.

I pedal home with my hood up and listening to the wonderful "Fingers of Love" by Crowded House.

Two Fat Ladies and *The Sound of Music*

SEPTEMBER 9TH, 2020.

Today my mum is eighty-eight years old. Eight years since the new hips arrived and the International Space Station flew over in celebration. Simon, Mum, Dad and I are all sitting in the lounge looking down at my mum's new pink and glittery Skechers shoes as she waggles them on the end of her outstretched legs. Her feet appear to be enjoying the attention of the room. "Who bought them for me?" she asks.

"We did," says Simon. "It's your birthday!"

"It isn't, is it?" she says with surprise. "Well, how old am I?"

In the style of a bingo caller, Simon says, "Two fat ladies eighty-eight!"

"What a cheek," says the birthday girl, laughing. "I'm not a fat lady, and I'm certainly not eighty-eight!"

Turning to my dad quizzically, "Well now I know he's lying! How old am I really, Guy?"

My dad says, "Well you were born in 1932, so if I'm doing the maths right you must be about a hundred and twenty." This makes us all laugh.

"Don't be daft," she says, looking down at her shoes, which appear to be tapping along to some imagined music.

"Look at my pink shoes – where did they come from?"

"Us," I say. "It's your birthday; we bought them for you."

She looks at my dad and Simon quizzically, looking for confirmation.

"It's true, eighty-eight today!" says Simon, adding, "Eighty-eight two fat ladies."

Simon has painted her nails to match her Skechers, and she is showing them off with outstretched arms and fingers.

I reflect over the last eight years. So much has happened, but I would say that, despite some clear deterioration in Mum's condition, there has been very little if any deterioration in her quality of life. Overall, we are all still managing to live amazingly well with it. As the rollercoaster of good times and tough times has continued, led by Mum, we have done our best to be with her in the moment, take things one day at a time, and trust that people are kind. At times things have been so settled that we have slipped into a kind of belief that her Alzheimer's has not and will not progress. It has just remained in a steady state with no obvious signs of worsening, and this has enabled us all to just get on with life and not worry too much about it. Then occasionally and unexpectedly it has risen out of nowhere and shown its strength, stamped its feet and insisted on being taken seriously and respected. Every time this has happened, it has shaken us, but, like the earth tremor in San Francisco, it hasn't managed to knock us over. The earth shakes, but we hold each other up and move on.

We are all loving this. We have had dinner, a birthday cake with candles, a bottle or two of Lambrini, and all to the soundtrack of Nat King Cole crooning in the background. We also have Christmas crackers, but I'm not sure why. I found them in a cupboard – it isn't the best idea as Mum is still not convinced it's her birthday and the crackers almost prove her right. However, they did give her the opportunity to, once again, read out the jokes. I noticed she needs a little more prompting now, but she can still read well, and we all laughed at the jokes, which seem to get worse each year.

Dad and I move to the other end of the lounge and sit in

armchairs. Simon and Mum stay put at the table, concentrating on a crossword. This is a relatively new activity; it's always just the two of them, but they need us as an audience – they are laughing, cheating, squeezing in more letters than they should and making up new words – it's like they are putting on a show and audience participation is unavoidable.

Simon: "Three across – what seven-letter word struck an iceberg on its maiden voyage and sank on the 15 April 1912? First three letters T-I-T?"

"T-I-T," repeats Mum, "spells tit."

We momentarily find ourselves on the set of yet another *Carry On* film.

"What can it be, Guy?" she asks.

Simon repeats the question, and we have another *Carry On* moment. "HMS Tit?" says my Dad.

Catching Mum's eye, I mouth the answer to her in an exaggerated conspiratorial way. She announces, "I know, I know – it's Gigantic!"

Simon laughs, "But where's the tit in gigantic?" This provokes yet another wave of sniggers.

Making my way through to the kitchen, I pass Mum and whisper in her ear, "Titanic!"

She enjoys these not-so-secret manoeuvres, but, not hearing me properly, she says, "What is it?" I repeat my fly past in my now loud whisper. Her face lights up. "I know, I know, Titanic!" We all cheer her. She loves the cheating and the attention; turning to Simon, she asks, "What is Titanic?" He tells her it's a ship that sank in 1912 but points out that he doesn't know how to spell it.

This is a nudge for her to help. He slowly says the word, breaking it into syllables.

"Ti-tan-ic." She repeats back to him and then spells, "T-I-T-A-N-I-C." Perfect spelling; no surprises there.

With amazing insight, my mum says quietly to Simon,

"It's funny you know; I can't remember what day it is, but I can spell Titanic!"

Simon then asks her what the Titanic is. "It's that ship that sunk and drowned all those people of course!" Then she goes on to embellish the story in hushed tones for Simon's ears only. This woman is amazing; despite her dementia, she has still managed to deliver the goods and provide the correct spelling and a detailed, slightly made-up story of the icy tragedy...all with a bit of help and cheating, of course – a family tradition.

DECEMBER 18TH, 2020.

"Is it really Christmas? It doesn't feel like it," says Mum.

"Once the tree's up it will," replies Simon. "What's your favourite Christmas music, Renee?"

"Carols from King's College Cambridge," she replies with no hesitation. Simon puts on the stereo. There follows an afternoon of her singing along with *Carols* – remarkably she has retained all the words – while directing the decoration of the tree for the first time in her new house and telling us the story behind each ornament. She is in her element and, just like when we populated her showcase earlier in the year, she is enjoying having the opportunity to be creative and in charge of the proceedings.

Later that evening we are eating mince pies, and listening to *Ella Wishes You a Swinging Christmas*. We reminisce about the past, and all agree that it does indeed feel Christmasy.

DECEMBER 26TH, 2020. BOXING DAY

Unfortunately, my brother Martin and his partner Helen couldn't come to stay for the holidays because of the Covid-19 restrictions. Mum and Dad, both being in their eighties, are more vulnerable to the virus and the risk is too great. But we have managed to make the most of the situation by FaceTiming as a family a couple of times, so it has felt like we are together.

We shifted Christmas Day to Boxing Day because Simon needed to go to work, and he is not only an essential part of any family gathering but also head chef. He cooks an amazing Christmas dinner, which is well worth delaying by twenty-four hours. Now, in the evening, we sit in the lounge chatting about another planned trip down to Exmouth in the spring to visit Jessie and Roy. Mum is feeling positive about this holiday because the excitement of seeing these cherished friends far outweighs any concerns she may have about where we will stay, what we shall eat, etc. She knows she is in safe and risk-free hands with us, but I'm pretty sure that when the departure date draws closer, she will become preoccupied with the details and perceived risks. Anyway, tonight we are having a good time with our cracker hats, bellies full of food, and drinks flowing.

A little later, having enjoyed her day, Mum says she is tired and is ready for bed, so she and my dad stand up to go to their house, next door to ours. Suddenly she lets out a scream and immediately needs to sit down. She tries to stand again but is in excruciating pain in her hip and right leg. The pain is so strong she quickly has tears in her eyes and can barely move. Being a determined soul, she gives it a few minutes and then decides to hold onto a chair and tries to loosen up her joint by swinging her leg back and forth, far more practical thinking than anything I could muster up.

Eventually, taking tiny painful steps and with the support of my dad and Simon, she manages to make her way next door and, amazingly, up the stairs to bed. This experience is traumatic, not just for her but for all of us. Once she is settled, the three of us sit downstairs and have a cup of tea. It feels like we are in shock. We are not used to seeing Mum in pain or in tears, and we are all shaken and emotional about what has just happened. One moment we were about to say goodnight after a lovely Boxing Day and then, with no warning or indication that anything was amiss, everything changed. Trying to contain the situation and prevent our imaginations taking us into a dark place, we drink our tea and spend some time reassuring each other that, once the painkillers have taken effect and she has had a good night's sleep, the pain will have subsided and everything will be OK.

One of the consequences of her short-term memory loss is that if Mum doesn't feel the leg pain in the morning, it is highly unlikely that she will have any memory of what has taken place. In addition to this, by then, any residual emotions left over from the experience are likely to be short-lived or non-existent. This is a kind of silver lining, which, on several occasions, has helped her to recover and move forwards quickly following any illness or injury. For example, a few years ago, while rushing along a pavement late for a Johnny Mathis concert, Mum tripped and fell forwards, breaking some bones in her wrist. As a result of this, rather than enjoying an evening of crooning and rekindling any possible romance between herself and Mr. Mathis, she underwent complex surgery and had a plate screwed into her wrist. Speaking to her on the phone just a couple of days later, she didn't even mention the accident or ensuing surgery. There was no pain to remind her, so it had slipped her mind. Of course, when I brought it up, she very much enjoyed the praise I was heaping on her, and then she went on to tell me a long tale about the surgeon knowing she had worked for the NHS and making an extra fuss of her, which included giving her some strong tablets "normal patients" couldn't have.

Tonight, Simon, Dad, and I all head to our beds hoping that a good night's sleep will do the trick, there will be no pain, and the incident will be forgotten.

DECEMBER 27TH, 2020.

So here we are. Mum and I sitting upstairs in her bedroom watching *The Sound of Music* on a small television and waiting for an ambulance. I am perched on the end of the bed, and she is sitting, a little uncomfortably, in a compact armchair. Unfortunately, the pain hasn't gone away as we hoped. If anything, it seems to have magnified and, despite our efforts, there is no way she can get down the stairs.

We are all emotionally and physically exhausted. Today has been such a long day, waiting and waiting, with Mum not being able to move or comprehend what is going on. Dad, Simon, and I have been taking it in turns to sit with her in the bedroom. Now it's my turn once again, and I am struggling to convince her that we have done the right thing by calling an ambulance and reassure her that everything will be fine. To be honest, I'm not even convincing myself, and knowing me well, she can see right through the positive story I am spinning.

Although she is virtually immobile, she is adamant that she does not need to go to a hospital and certainly doesn't need an ambulance. I explain that our reason for calling an ambulance is that earlier on, even with our help, she couldn't get down the stairs without screaming out in agony. She doesn't believe me as she can't remember us even trying. She is getting angry, and I don't blame her. I can tell that she feels something is being done *to* her rather than *with* her, and she is highly suspicious and anxious. She is preoccupied with trying to understand what is happening and she desperately wants to take some control. I can understand this. It seems like everyone's opinion counts apart from hers.

She feels disempowered, and she is struggling to retain the details of why we have been sitting here waiting for an ambulance for over twelve hours and why everyone except her feels that this is the right thing to do. As a result of this, Mum has become agitated and is repeating her questions over and over again. When I remind her about her leg pain, she challenges what I'm saying because, as she is sitting still, she can't feel any pain at all, so I must be trying to deceive her. This is so difficult as our relationship is built on love and trust – but she is convinced I am not telling the truth.

* * *

The Sound of Music has played a small but significant role in our relationship. Some of the songs, especially "Edelweiss," have been part of our soundtrack from as far back as I can remember. Mum took me to see the film at the cinema when I was far too young to understand what was going on. I enjoyed the singing and loved the yodelling goats' puppet show, but I was terrified by the scene down in the crypt of the convent, the one where Rolf discovers the von Trapp family hiding amongst the sarcophagi and is deciding whether to let them go free and escape over the mountains or blow his whistle and alert the Nazis. I still find this scene scary and disturbing. It's all so threatening and makes me think that even in the face of overwhelming danger and threat, individual decisions and actions can have an impact on outcomes.

Although I am still finding this difficult to watch, particularly given the threatening circumstances we have found ourselves in today, my mum has been distracted by Julie Andrews and is now telling me about the war. She, at last, has something to take her mind away from what is going on and why we are 'trapped' upstairs in the bedroom, and instead focus on telling me about a significant part of her life. She launches into the legend of the two bombs. Being influenced by the film, she then tells me that as she, her mum, dad and sister sat together in their makeshift air raid shelter, wondering if the house had been destroyed, they sang "Edelweiss" and some hymns to ask for God's help.

Then thankfully, a little light relief and distraction. The von Trapps are heading over the mountains and Maria is singing her heart out. It's amazing how this happy ending and joyful singing has lifted our spirits and brightened the room. Mum sings along with "Climb Every Mountain." This is yet another example of the impact of her condition; it's just amazing how she is struggling to remember why she is going to the hospital, but she can remember all the words to a song she hasn't heard in years.

I attempt to sing along, but those high notes are a challenge; she laughs at my efforts and is now all smiles. Then falling silent and caught up in the wedding scene, with the rays of sunlight shining through a majestic stained-glass window and the choir singing songs we know. I can see that she is moved by this, and it reminds me of our visit to the cathedral in Chichester back in the summer. Once again, the soundtrack of our lives, along with Mum's faith, has lifted the mood, and just for a few minutes we have a little nugget of fun. It takes a raised awareness and conscious effort to recognise and value these small events and live in the moment, at a time like this.

Part Five

Night, Night, Sleep Tight, and Remember... Don't Let the Bed Bugs Bite!

JANUARY 4TH, 2021.

Today is my birthday. Me, Dad, and Simon are speaking to Mum using FaceTime on the hospital ward's iPad. It's wonderful that in these days of lockdown and isolation that the NHS has provided these devices to enable people to stay connected with their loved ones. Mum is sitting up in bed. The nurse is showing her how to hold the iPad so we can see her face, but she seems to be waving it about, giving us a view of the top of her head, the polished floor and then her neighbour in the next bed. Eventually we have a close-up of her nose and then her beautiful smiling face. She has hardly ever done this before but seems to take it for granted that she can see and speak to us.

"Hello, Mum, it's Marcus, it's my birthday and I'm fifty-seven years old today."

"Is it!? Happy birthday, darlin'."

"Do you remember how you were feeling fifty-seven years ago?" I enquire.

"Relieved you were out, I imagine," she says with a smile. I can tell the nurse is still with her just off camera and she, ever the entertainer, is making him laugh with her comments.

"How does it feel to know that your youngest son is fifty-seven?" I ask.

"You're not that old, are you? Is he messing me about, Guy?"

"Yep," he confirms. "He's been messing us about for fifty-seven years, but it feels much longer to me."

She is laughing, then quick as a flash, "Well, if he's fifty-seven, how old am I?"

"Two fat ladies, eighty-eight," says Simon.

I don't know how loud the volume is on the iPad, but we can hear giggles on the hospital ward. She is, of course, grabbing the opportunity to hold court. It must be a funny conversation to listen in to, not your regular birthday chit chat. It's so nice to see her smile; she has been in hospital for over a week, and due to Covid-19 we are not allowed to visit her. This is very difficult for all of us to deal with, especially my dad, who is illogically but understandably struggling with guilt about the situation. He is missing the woman he loves and has spent every day with for over sixty years.

My emotions are also running high. I am constantly telling myself that she is in the right place. But I am not so sure. The doctors don't seem to be able to find out what the problem is, so with no treatment there appears to be no improvement; time ticks on, and no diagnosis to date. And, of course, the virus, which is now rampant around the world, adds an extra dimension and risk, meaning this is not a good time to be in hospital.

My dad has had his Covid-19 vaccination, but my mum has missed hers due to being hospitalised. I assumed she would have it in there, but apparently vaccines are not being administered in hospitals. From the outside this doesn't seem to make any sense – surely the risk of infection is increased in hospital. This adds to our concerns, but we decide to trust the system. In fact, we have no choice. The whole situation must be overwhelming for the doctors and nurses. However, the good news is that the hospital is divided into green and red areas and wards, indicating Covid status. Red is for patients who have tested positive for the virus, and green is for those who have not. This simple and sensible approach minimises the risk of cross-contamination. Thankfully, my mum is on a green ward, she is Covid-free, which is reassuring, and I have to remind myself that there are people in the hospital who are in a far worse situation than us.

It's a mad time – the TV and internet are obsessed with death tolls. It feels like a war, and I suppose it is. Seeing anyone in a public building with no face mask or standing too close to the next person is shocking. Sneezing in public is not that far removed from firing a gun! It's amazing how we have adjusted to this new world in such a short time. There are new parameters to how we interact as a society, how we travel, how we learn and how we work.

* * *

It's three in the afternoon, and I am wondering why Mum is in bed and wearing her nightie. I don't ask her; she is not a child, and I don't want to treat her like one, and I'm proud to say she wouldn't stand for it anyway. But one of her lifelong mantras is hovering in my mind: "If you don't use it, you lose it." This is something she has said to me many, many times, and it was her motivation for making such a speedy recovery from her hip replacements. She knew that if she didn't work for her new hips, meaning exercising them every day, then they certainly wouldn't work for her. She has never been ill enough to stay in bed, and despite the situation I am still surprised that this seems to be the case now.

I ask her what she's been up to – is she getting about and meeting people?

"Yes, of course," she replies. "I get out of bed after the doctor does his rounds every morning. I wait because I don't want to get in his way, and I've spent my entire working life with doctors, so I know how busy they are, and they don't like to be disturbed."

She continues, "I mean I was there when the NHS was first set up in 1948. Before that, it was the National Insurance Committee." She is proudly telling us about working in the office for the NHS, knowing all the top doctors and them calling her *Renee Darlin'*. Mum is enjoying telling this story. Of course we have heard all of it hundreds, and maybe thousands, of times in the past, and why not? She is proud of who she is and what she has achieved. She is confirming her identity to anyone who is listening. We are responding with a hint of admiration and pride in our voices, widening her smile and boosting her confidence, which is probably doing her as much good as any medication she may be taking.

"So once the doctors have done their rounds, what do you get up to?" I ask.

"Well," she says, "I get dressed, put on my lippy and go and have a chat with the doctors and nurses. Then I talk to the other ladies on the ward. There are some poor old souls here; it's sad really, no family visiting them."

My dad, realising that some of those *poor old souls* may be able to hear what she is saying, changes the subject and asks how her leg is.

"What do you mean my leg? I've got two legs, and both are fine; the doctor told me I am fit and well, and he said not to let anyone tell me I'm not." She continues telling us what she does in the daytime and also about all the goings on in the evenings and overnight.

After the call, we are reflecting that she hasn't lost any of her spirit, she is continuing her lifelong insistence that she is fit and well – and who are we to argue with that?

JANUARY 5TH, 2021.

Every day since my mum went into hospital, I phone the ward to find out how she's doing, and today is no exception. Despite her confusion about the reason for her hospitalisation, and her insistence that she is fit and well, I am feeling pretty positive about yesterday's conversation. She was certainly in good spirits and, ever curious, enjoying the comings and goings on the ward. At least we know she is getting up and dressed and moving about, which is crucial, even if she was in bed at three in the afternoon.

I speak to the duty nurse and find myself telling my mum's story. I describe her memory issues and confusion. Then I go on to talk about her likes and dislikes, what she enjoys talking about, her tendency to give people, especially medical people, the answers she thinks they are looking for, and how she is motivated by positive, reinforcing compliments and feedback.

I have repeated this story at least once a day since she was taken into hospital. In fact, on day one, I wrote it all down and gave it to the ambulance crew, who said they would make sure it stayed with her and was added to her notes. This didn't happen, and although each time I tell the story, the person on the other end of the line assures me that they have written it all down for all the staff to read. The truth is that either it isn't recorded, the notes aren't read, or the staff are so overwhelmed in the face of the pandemic that this just isn't a priority. However, my strategy is to keep repeating myself, just like my mum, in the hope that at least the person I speak to will bear this in mind when they are with her and make it count.

I ask the nurse about how Mum gets dressed and out of bed, what kind of support she needs. "She hasn't got out of bed and been dressed since she was admitted; in fact she hasn't really moved at all other than when she is being transferred to use the commode so she can be washed and have her bedclothes changed."

Dad, Simon, and I are stunned, and more than a little concerned by this revelation. After all, we are talking about a fellow wildebeest here, a woman who just can't stop moving.

Later the same day I'm speaking to an occupational therapist who is helpful and positive but tells me it is a struggle to get Mum to move out of bed. I suggest he gives her positive praise for the progress she made yesterday, and to tell her that all the doctors are really pleased about it. I know this is a small lie, but I think it's our best shot. Realising that the therapist has no idea about my mum's condition and memory issues, I tell the story again. He says the information is really useful and he will add it to her notes.

JANUARY 12TH, 2021.

As well as phoning the hospital at least once a day to have any updates, we also manage to speak to Mum on FaceTime regularly. The nursing staff are being so helpful, sorting out the iPad and agreeing a time for us to call. They are getting to know her, and we can tell she is enjoying the attention. There has been no progress with her leg pain. Their original thinking, that it could be sciatica, has come to nothing and now they are talking about discharging her back home and providing some equipment to help her get about. Although this is the best option and we want to get her back as soon as possible, it's also worrying, especially for my dad.

The plan leaves us with more questions than answers, but at least we have something to channel our energy into. So, we are converting the lounge into a bedroom, with a TV and commode. There is no downstairs toilet, but we are already exploring having a stairlift put in. However, my mum is an active and physically independent person, so how will she cope? Maybe living downstairs in the lounge could be the motivation she needs to get moving? I hope so. I can imagine her saying "Right, I'm off to bed!" and just heading up the stairs with no fuss.

It has been sixteen days since we last saw her in the flesh. Visits are still not an option, and this is taking its toll. What started out as a sudden and severe pain in her leg that prevented her from being able to walk or climb stairs seems to be spiralling into a life-changing condition that has no name and could severely impact both of my parents' quality of life. I truly believe that her physicality, her ability to move around in the world and connect and interact with people and nature has played a crucial role in her ability to live well with dementia. So, this threat to the equilibrium is real, and difficult to come to terms with.

JANUARY 14TH, 2021.

"Hello, Mum, how are you today?"

"I'm fit and well, thank you. The doctors and nurses are very pleased with me. I've been walking about the ward today and have just got in bed for a lay down."

She's not lying to us; this is her reality, and it would be unhelpful to challenge what she is saying. She would be astounded if she knew that she hadn't walked in over twenty days. In fact, she would downright deny it and she would be upset, seeing it as some kind of negative accusation.

I have lost count of how many times I have told Mum's story to different professionals at the hospital. I have also offered to email a one-page profile to them several times but have been reassured that it's really not necessary as her notes are being updated.

I am on automatic – on repeat – feeling unheard. Once again, I can relate to how my mum must feel a lot of the time.

JANUARY 18TH, 2021.

I am on the telephone speaking to the nurse for an update. She tells me that Mum has been moved to a different ward. This isn't surprising as she has already been moved a couple of times. She is helpful and gives me the name of the ward and the number I need to call. I ask her how Mum has been, and she says she has been much the same, in good spirits but immobile. She then mentions that she has noticed that Mum seems to be forgetful and repeats herself a lot. I remain calm. "As I have said before, my mum is living with dementia..."

While I am speaking, my dad walks in and I catch his eye. I can immediately tell that something is wrong. He interrupts my conversation, "I have just had a text from the hospital saying that Renee has tested positive for Covid-19."

"No, that's not the case," I reassure him. "I'm on the phone to them now."

The nurse can hear our conversation, and I check with her just to be sure.

"Yes, your mum has the virus; that's why she has been moved to a red ward."

The fist of fear immediately appears and starts to grow in my chest, its fingers pushing through my ribs, reaching up to my neck and throat.

My dad is in shock, as is Simon.

What does this mean?

What now?

I ask what the prognosis is – I'm told that she may well make a full recovery and it's not a concern until people have had it for eleven days. This gives us some solace. She is receiving the treatment she needs to best overcome the virus, so all we can hope is that her drive not to be controlled by any illness will once again kick and pull her through.

JANUARY 26TH, 2021.

I am speaking to a doctor. He says that Mum's health is really suffering with Covid-19. In fact, it's so bad it seems to be affecting her short-term memory, and she is repeating herself. I swallow my frustration and quickly tell her story. But my real concern is how the virus is affecting her. Other than the short-term memory issue, which has nothing to do with Covid-19, what else is happening and is this a concern? He tells me it is serious, she is becoming breathless, but she is strong and could recover.

Later I try and organise for us to FaceTime her, but she is sleeping so we leave her to rest.

JANUARY 27TH, 2021.

The phone rings. I answer and the caller says, "Your mum's health has declined, and if you want to say goodbye to her you need to do it today. If you want to visit you can, but, due to restrictions, we can only allow one person in for a limited time."

The wind rushes out of my lungs, and I feel like I have been punched in the stomach.

I sink into a kind of fog. How has this happened? How did we go from planning her return home to this inconceivable situation in just a few days?

The nurse is telling me all sorts of things and I think I am asking questions, but I can't really take anything onboard. I am unable to understand what is being said. It's like I have a giant blanket wrapped around my head muffling her words. I just have one sentence repeating on full blast in a huge, dark, empty echo chamber – which is my mind:

"If you want to say goodbye to her, you need to do it today."

I'm overwhelmed and can't really understand what is happening. I mumble some comment to end the conversation and put the phone down. Silence.

I tell Simon, and he helps me calm down and make some sort of sense of what is happening. "You need to tell your dad." I go next door and ring the doorbell. My poor dad.

* * *

Later that day, we are driving along the seafront to the hospital. Avoiding the overwhelming magnitude of what is taking place, we bypass our emotions by focusing our conversation on random and practical things. We are talking about traffic lights and how when pedestrians press the button to cross, the lights don't seem to change for ages; why is that? Then we talk about the kitesurfers who are braving the January waves, and we even joke about that time Simon was blown off towards France and had to be rescued by the lifeboat. I then ramble on about my friend Barney who kitesurfs in Australia. We are facing one of the most challenging situations in our lives, and we are relying on small talk to keep a lid on it!

The hospital comes into view, and we are suddenly quiet, each of us trying to come to terms with what is about to happen.

I am still attempting to process the concept of saying goodbye to my mum. I don't think I can do that. What would she think? Is she aware? How can I say goodbye to somebody I have known all my life? How can my dad say goodbye to the love of his life? I look at him, crumpled in his seat deep in thought and trying to hold it together.

We park at the hospital. We haven't even acknowledged that only one of us can go and see her. My dad can't go alone; I need to be there for him, and I also need to see my lovely mum...for the last time?... Surely not.

Simon is also struggling. He and Mum are very close. They have developed a deep and loving relationship, with a kind of secret understanding, as if they speak a slightly different language when they are together. Always giggling and whispering. He is a hero, he proves this on a regular basis, but today he really does something wonderful. He goes into the hospital ahead of us and a few minutes later gives us the news that we will all be able to see her. First, he will go in and spend some time with her, and then Dad and I will go in together. I don't know how he made this happen, but he did, and for that, we will be eternally grateful.

Dad and I are sitting in a waiting room – numb, but relieved we are together. Simon has disappeared off to see Mum, apparently and inconceivably, for the last time. The situation is very intense and almost impossible to take onboard. Inside I am overwhelmed and feel as if I'm not really a part of it. It's like I'm watching two other people sitting in a waiting room. Despite these feelings, we, once again, spend our time talking about practical everyday stuff, trying to normalise or even ignore what is happening. Perhaps if we ignore it, it will go away.

Eventually our random conversation makes its way towards the issue we are facing – we are here to see Mum for the first time in nearly a month – we haven't all been together since the von Trapps escaped over the mountains. We do not even entertain the idea that this is the last time we will see her and apparently, we are here to say goodbye.

Simon is back, looking relaxed and peaceful. He smiles. "You will be surprised – she's OK, you will be OK, everything is fine." They had spent twenty minutes together, making small talk and connecting in the way they always do.

"Hello darlin'!"

"Hello Renee, you are looking beautiful..."

Despite his reassurance, I can't imagine it being OK at all, but we are clinging onto his comment like a life raft. As we stand up and head off, my emotions are running high, and I cannot even start to consider what this is like for my poor dad. While slowly making our way down the corridor to her ward, we are talking about Mum's knowledge and emotions in relation to the situation. Simon had said she seemed to be aware that she was in hospital and, he felt, aware that she was dying. And we are trying to get our heads around how she might be feeling. This difficult question quickly leads us to discussing her faith.

Since her childhood, Mum has kept very solid religious beliefs, which are not complicated. She believes that God is the creator. Jesus, his son, was born on Earth to show us how to live a good and holy life, and he died for us all.

We remind ourselves that she truly believes that when her time comes, she will be reunited with her dear old Mum and Dad, her sister, her friends, and at some point in the future we will be together again as a family. This ingrained belief means she has never expressed any fear of death, and she certainly doesn't see it as the end, but rather as a kind of reunion and new beginning. This short but powerful conversation isn't planned. It has just come to us by chance, but it seems to be providing both of us with a kind of calming strength and connection, a tangible anchor to hold on to in this unimaginable situation.

As instructed, we put on our protective masks, aprons, and gloves to minimise risk of cross contamination. There is something of an Apollo mission about this, and for a fleeting moment those fabulous wives and their handbags cross my mind. I catch a reflection of us in a window and think of "Pigs in Space" on *The Muppet Show* – I mention it to my dad.

Why did I say that? Trying to normalise and bring humour into the most emotionally charged moments we have ever experienced together? It doesn't matter. He is oblivious to my comments; he is in his own world, trying to process this unexpected and overwhelming event.

It seems so counter-intuitive that our last moments together with Mum will be absent of any skin-on-skin physical touch.

As we make our way along a corridor, we glimpse her through an internal window. She looks tired and a little dishevelled, but as we walk in, she sees us, and her face lights up. I am relieved she recognises us through all the pandemic regalia, and she is clearly pleased to see us.

Although she has a deep cough that is irritating her, and is frustrated by an oxygen mask that clearly wasn't designed for comfort, it still doesn't make her look or sound like a person who is close to the end of her life. She still has that familiar spark. It's like her spirit and life force, and to be honest, probably her stubbornness, is fighting its way through and insisting we will have a normal conversation. She is chatting away about the doctors, nurses, and other patients. She knows she is in hospital, but there is no mention of why. There is also no mention of the outfits we all find ourselves wearing. The only acknowledgement being her pulling off her oxygen mask.

Although a little frail, she is exuding a reassuring confidence that everything will be OK – for us and for her.

We are here to say goodbye and, looking into her eyes, we can see she knows this on some level, but there certainly isn't a feeling of permanence or finality about it.

Mum is thirsty and needs help to raise the cup up to her lips to take sips of water. Becoming more lucid, she is telling us that the doctors and nurses knew she used to work for the NHS. It's heartening to think that even in this challenging situation it is still important for her to confirm her identity and what she is proud of.

Then she starts talking about family. How are Martin and Helen? I mention that they have been ill with Covid-19 so can't come down and visit.

"What is that?" she asks.

I tell her about the virus. "Oh dear, that must be awful for them," she says, clearly unaware or having forgotten that she also has it herself. In fact, it's obvious she is unaware what Covid-19 is. After all, it doesn't sound like an illness; it sounds like the kind of car a boy racer would drive.

She asks what we are having for dinner on Sunday. "I don't

know, what do you fancy?" says my dad.

"Roast chicken!" says Mum, and it is agreed.

Then she tells us that the previous day she was lying in her bed looking up at the ceiling, and she saw a beautiful blue sky. She elaborates and says she could feel the warmth of the sun on her skin and see birds flying high above her head.

Then she says, "I also saw my mum and dad, after all these years, and they were smiling and waving at me."

* * *

Too soon, it's time to go; my dad is holding his wife's hand. We each kiss her on the cheek, skin to skin.

We don't say goodbye.

* * *

Later in the evening, the phone rings and I am told by the nurse that they are stopping Mum's medication. I guess this is why we were asked to come and say goodbye. And would explain why she seemed so...fit and well?

I don't know how I am supposed to respond.

JANUARY 28TH, 2021.

6:30 a.m.

We are in bed asleep when my mobile phone rings. It's the hospital. A voice tells me that Mum passed away at 6:20 a.m.

It doesn't seem possible that the person who was full of life and overflowing with love yesterday has now died.

We have lost her.

Part Six

Dancing in the Dark

When I lived in Cornwall, one of my favourite things to do was ride my bike at night. I would head out through the high sided lanes with the light on my handlebars illuminating a small globe in front of me. Reaching the highest point of the windswept Penwith Peninsular, I could see the lights of both St Ives and Penzance, coast to coast, where the English Channel meets the Atlantic Ocean. If it was a clear night, the ride was magical. Ancient landscapes, crystal stars, standing stones, sweeping beams from a lighthouse, and twinkling ships making their way to who knows where.

Tonight in 2022, almost forty years later, I am out under a clear and crisp night sky again, but this time I am running, and I am in Sussex, with a view over the English Channel. I enjoy the nocturnal life. Whether it's reading, walking, running, or pedaling, I have always appreciated the *otherness* of nighttime. It's like somebody has pressed pause on normal life, and another quieter, more contented population of people and animals take over the world for the night shift. Time passes at a different pace, leaving room for thought and, if you're lucky, freedom to enjoy what is happening in the moment. My run is slow and methodical. I sense the heightened feeling of isolation and space that comes with darkness. I have no music in my ears, and I am far more alert to the world around me than I would be in daylight. But, inside my head there is room for my mind to explore issues, expand my thinking, and to see things more clearly.

As I run, I am thinking about the comments my mum made when we were sitting in Chichester Cathedral. When she spoke about her experience of being in sacred buildings and spaces and how they have the same familiar spiritual and sensory impact wherever you are in the world, and whatever your beliefs. She went on to say that this meant that it was always possible to connect, recharge and gain strength when needed. I also think about our final conversation, when she told us she had seen a blue sky above her hospital bed with flying birds, a warm sun, and her parents. It's clear that although she loved being in physical sacred spaces, she didn't need to be in them to be able to connect with her faith and spirituality. Her mind and her beliefs were her own internal sacred place, and it is her faith – her truth – that has proved to be a great comfort to myself, my dad, and our family through the most difficult times in the buildup and aftermath of her passing. Once again, we have joined Mum in her truth and have benefited no end from the experience.

I could not be described as a particularly religious person. I do not sign up to one faith above another, and I do not attend any place of worship. But, right here, right now, as I run along the coast path in a steady state, I am reminded that when I find myself in this situation, being physically active at night, in the dark, under the stars, or when I am swimming in the sea, I do feel a heightened connection to something bigger. Something that is energising, inspiring, and everywhere. This feeling could be due to the impact exercise-related endorphins have on my brain, or maybe it's something else, something that I can't quite describe without using the same language my mum used when she spoke about her beliefs.

I reach my turning point, and lean both hands on a tree to stretch a twinging calf muscle. To ensure the stretch is effective, I not only need to adopt the right posture and concentrate on physically increasing the length of the muscle, but I also need to visualise the muscle stretching and relaxing. If I don't visualise what is taking place under my skin, then the twinge will undoubtedly return. I then change sides and stretch the other calf – it's good to balance these things out. As I do this, I notice my breathing is slowing down. My heart and lungs have clearly been working hard, but in just sixty or seventy seconds of pushing on a tree they are already recovering and returning to a resting rate. I feel a breeze catch the sweat on the back of my neck. I'd better start moving before I begin to get chilly. I set off, retracing my footsteps, and casting a long shadow from a bright moon that has risen over my left shoulder. My calf pain is gone and forgotten, and, in a few minutes, I find I have once again achieved a comfortable rhythm and pace.

I think about the important role regular physical activity has in my life. It is the constant that plays a big part in helping me keep not only my physical, but also my mental health in check. That does not mean I don't have my struggles; I certainly do, but it does mean I am doing something proactive, that improves my feelings of self-worth and my ability to connect with other people. I also think about the role it has played in relation to my mum's dementia.

Regular exercise has given me the time to think about what has been happening, what we have learnt, where we are now, and what we need to do to safeguard the future. This respite and disconnection has enabled me, overall, to be there in the moment, for both of my parents whenever possible. I really hope my dad has been able to have that same space and time for a similar experience; I think he has achieved this by spending time gardening and, until the last six months of Mum's life, going off to work two days a week. It was just a few hours each of those days, but it did give him the opportunity to think about something different and talk to his friends.

I slow down and walk for a bit. Out to sea there is a blanket of hundreds of flashing red lights levitating between the water and the stars, each one attached to an invisible giant wind turbine, making renewable energy from natural elements. I think about our windmill back in Clacton, a beacon guiding us home.

High above I spot a tiny satellite following its lonely path across the sky. Lou Reed's "Satellite of Love" starts to play in my mind, and I imagine Renee up there somewhere reunited with her parents and loved ones.

As I walk down to the water's edge, the coming dawn is faintly changing the tones on the horizon, black to blue to pink. Then, in the corner of my eye, I detect another moving object, most likely a satellite. I watch it for a short while then notice a slight flash and I realise it's an aircraft cruising at a very high altitude in an arc across the sky. It amazes me to think that this tiny insignificant flashing speck probably contains at least three hundred people, all living their lives at the centre of their universes, looking for adventure, new chapters, fresh starts, belonging, and love. I wonder where it's going. It's travelling from east to west, heading in the same direction as the plane we waved off from Heathrow all those years ago. So much has happened since then.

Feeling a cold breeze, I make my way up the beach and start a slow jog. At first, I'm plodding with heavy cold legs, but after a few minutes I find my stride and am once again moving with a smooth rhythm, not pretty but not plodding. It's been fifteen years since that plane and our visitors left the runway, fifteen years since the couple in the airport had an affair, and fifteen years since the nun with slightly scuffed shoes left the convent and shacked up with a handsome single dad.

Back then we were at the beginning of our journey into a world of dementia. A new, mysterious, scary and, at times, a surprisingly joyful chapter for all of us. At that time my mum was desperately trying to keep a grip on her life and protect her identity and her pride, while we, her loved ones, were doing our best to support her to do this. We did not always get it right but, at the very least, we learnt from our mistakes and improved over time. Thinking about it, that has been the story ever since. The combination of her determination to live her best life, along with my dad's unwavering commitment to supporting her to do so, has been a constant driving force, keeping us all on track and focused on our simple goal: to ensure that right now, in the moment, life is as good as it can be.

While thinking about this, I have been running on autopilot. Moving forwards through landscape, space, and time, literally taking it in my stride at a pace that suits me. I assume I have also unconsciously been bypassing obstacles and hazards, avoiding broken glass and bottomless holes, and here I am still alive and having a lovely run. It occurs to me that this is a good metaphor for how we have all managed to get through the last fifteen years, taking it one step after another, avoiding hazards when possible and getting on with our lives.

* * *

During the last two years of Mum's life, the regularity and intensity of her confusion increased. At these times she seemed to have an in-built powerful current of energy focused solely on clearing the fog and making sense of the world around her. I never saw her sit back and just accept her confused state. Sometimes, this uncertainty would include her not recognising key people such as myself and my dad. Thankfully, this was a rare occurrence, but when it did happen it was tough. Back in the early days this issue would have been near the top of my list of fears – the *what ifs* – and it would have undoubtedly featured in my dad's list as well. But by the time it did happen, we had learnt that the progression of her illness was not linear or predictable, so although this experience was frightening for us, we knew it was very likely that later she would recognise us as usual, and I'm happy (and very lucky) to say that was usually the case. The key to dealing with these kinds of incidents was to keep it in perspective, not overreact, and just remember that she just wanted to know who we were so she could feel reassured that she was in the right place with the right people.

Thinking about these things, I feel a sudden and overwhelming pang of sadness. I slow down and sit on a bench – bizarrely I find myself pretending to stretch just in case somebody is out there in the darkness to witness what I'm doing. I'm not sure what has triggered these unexpected emotions; loss, pride, relief, grief, or just the fact that we have got to the end of an amazing and scary journey based on love and respect? I'm not sure; maybe all the above.

I am distracted by another sudden change, but this time it's a cold physical sensation. I realise I am sitting on a wet bench, and my backside is now soaked. I get the feeling Mum is looking down and laughing at me, and I think she's telling me to cheer up, get a grip and stop taking myself so seriously! I hope so.

As I head home, I run past the pier. A big flock of starlings roost in the structure below the boardwalk and above the water. The coming dawn light has woken them, and they are beginning to leave the roost in small groups, heading inland to find breakfast. I am reminded of the science behind their evening murmuration – each individual using the seven birds closest to it to navigate and effectively move with, and be a part of, the wider community. I can't help but see how this approach also enabled my mum to live her life to the full. She had about seven key people around her, who proactively enabled her to navigate her way through each day while also having fun, and in addition to this, she had the ongoing kindness of strangers, who never failed to welcome her into the wider community, and in doing so empowered her to fly.

Of course, if I said this to her, she would respond by saying, "Yes, but who taught the starlings how to fly..."

As always, she gets the last word.

138
STOP
DAVID HOCKNEY

Afterword

It's 2024, three years since Mum passed away. We are not sure what to think about '*moving on*' or '*closure*.' We have certainly moved on, but we appear to have taken her with us. She seems to be as present as she ever was – does that matter? No, not at all.

We are not wallowing in sadness or loss – we are getting on with our lives.

In her final months, Mum taught me how to make cheese, potato, and onion pie – her post-pub signature dish. In fact, she taught me several times. We went to a supermarket to buy the ingredients (if you were wondering, there is a clue in the name of the dish). Then together we shared the jobs of peeling and boiling potatoes, chopping the onions, grating cheese, and mixing it all together with a blob of butter, and pepper and salt. Sometimes she would remember each of these steps and other times I would subtly fill in the gaps for her. While we did this, she would invariably tell me stories of the war, parties in the bungalow, or her mum and dad. Before putting the dish in the oven, she would add her secret ingredient, which would really *cut the mustard* (there is another clue in there if you look for it), and hey presto! Renee's signature dish was ready to go. This is one of the many examples of her sharing her skills and knowledge and even teaching others – a rare experience for people living with dementia, I would imagine.

Now, to mark significant dates and anniversaries, I cook

this dish, and while we eat, we listen to Johnny Mathis and raise a glass to Renee.

* * *

My dad is now approaching his tenth decade. Ronnie the Jack Russell has left us and is by Mum's side, and Dad has a new pup in his life called Pip. She's a young Jack Russell rescue. To say she is energetic is an understatement – she is devoted to her new dad, and the feeling is mutual. They have carved out a strong bond and routine for themselves. Their relationship can be a little fraught at times, due to my dad putting so much love and care into his garden, and Pip putting so much love and care into wrecking it in blind pursuit of the neighbourhood squirrels.

I have given up the *red wine smile* and the *gin grin* – I found myself hiding bottles from Simon in the garden; could there be a more cliched sign that things needed to change?

Dad and I go out dog walking together most days. We have a local wildlife park with a lake, some spinneys and beautiful reed beds that, together, attract a fantastic array of waterfowl and wildlife. On Sunday mornings we have breakfast in either, Brooklands Café or The Laughing Dog.

My dad is still pushing himself with technology; banking, shopping and, most important, connecting with his friends. While I write this, Simon is helping him to erect his new greenhouse. Although he has transformed his garden since he and Mum moved in, he has big plans and needs a greenhouse to bring them to fruition. So, what with a Jack Russell puppy, and an ambitious gardening project, my dad is focused very much on the future, and I am happy to report that he still has no intention of letting his age dictate how he lives his life.

* * *

Thank you for reading our story; I hope you enjoyed it. Please take whatever is useful, mess around with it, and make it work for you and your loved ones – in the moment – where the magic happens.

Thank you also to everyone who made my mum's life such a joy, including friends and family, casual acquaintances, and also those many nameless kind people who don't realise they are a part of the story, like the young family on the beach who welcomed her enthusiasm despite her trashing the social distancing rules, the waiter in London who noticed her Chanel N°5 and made her feel fabulous all those years ago, and also the friendly and welcoming hairdressers in salons past and present who made her feel special and beautiful.

Thank you also to our fellow starlings, Simon, Mel, Nick, Martin and Helen.

But most of all thank you to Guy Batterbury, my dad, the true hero of this story, and to Renee Batterbury, my mum, for always reminding us that her illness did not define her. She was an interesting, loving, and entertaining person – who just happened to be living with dementia.

She was, and always will be, bigger than it.

The soundtrack to this book is "People Make the World Go Round" by The Stylistics... Go play it loud!

Wherever, Whatever, Have a Nice Day

Acknowledgements

Thank you to Shani Moyle, Julie Babb, and Guy Batterbury for being my first proofreaders and giving me the confidence to keep going.

Thanks also to Andrew Fawcett, Nick and Mel Bengtsson and the many other people, including my OD friends, who have offered encouragement and insight throughout the writing of this book.

A big thank you to the excellent people from Atmosphere Press – who helped me find my way when I couldn't see the wood for the trees.

Above all, thanks and love to Simon Kral, who regularly throws me a life jacket when I most need one and has been there for me always.

About Atmosphere Press

Founded in 2015, Atmosphere Press was built on the principles of Honesty, Transparency, Professionalism, Kindness, and Making Your Book Awesome. As an ethical and author-friendly hybrid press, we stay true to that founding mission today.

If you're a reader, enter our giveaway for a free book here:

SCAN TO ENTER
BOOK GIVEAWAY

If you're a writer, submit your manuscript for consideration here:

SCAN TO SUBMIT
MANUSCRIPT

And always feel free to visit Atmosphere Press and our authors online at atmospherepress.com. See you there soon!

Author Bio

Marcus Batterbury's career has followed a meandering and unpredictable path. Amongst other things he has worked as a bike messenger, fitness instructor, cleaner, waiter, teacher and trainer. He has also travelled the UK by way of a green and beautiful campervan and the world by way of trains, planes and bicycles.

Marcus lives on the south coast of England with his partner, Simon, and his dog, Milo.

https://marcusbatterbury.com/

www.ingramcontent.com/pod-product-compliance
Ingram Content Group UK Ltd.
Pitfield, Milton Keynes, MK11 3LW, UK
UKHW041940021125
464635UK00002B/33

9 798891 329225